more fabulous Beans

Barb Bloomfield

Book Publishing Company
Summertown, Tennessee

Cover design: Cynthia Holzapfel
Interior design: Gwynelle Dismukes
Photography: Warren Jefferson
Food Stylist: Barb Bloomfield

Published in the United States by
Book Publishing Company
P.O. Box 99
Summertown, TN 38483
1-888-260-8458

Printed in Canada

Bloomfield, Barb, 1950-
  More fabulous beans / Barb Bloomfield.
     p. cm.
  ISBN 1-57067-146-X
  1. Cookery (Beans) 2. Vegetarian cookery. I. Title.
TX803.B4B58 2004
641.6'565--dc22
                              2003022655

Calculations for the nutritional analyses in
this book are based on the average number
of servings listed with the recipes and the
average amount of an ingredient if a range is
called for. Calculations are rounded up to
the nearest gram. If two options for an
ingredient are listed, the first one is used.
Not included are fat used for frying (unless
the amount is specified in the recipe),
optional ingredients, or serving suggestions.

ISBN 1-57067-146-X

09 08   07 06 05 04   6 5 4 3 2 1

On the cover:
Summer Cannelloni with Veggies, page 153

Printed on recycled paper

The Book Publishing Co. is committed to preserving ancient forests and natural
resources. We have elected to print this title on Enviro Offset, which is 100%
postconsumer recycled and processed chlorine free. As a result of our paper
choice, we have saved the following natural resources:

45.6 trees (40 feet in height)
13,300 gallons of water
7,790 kwh of electricity
114 pounds of air pollution

We are a member of Green Press Initiative. For more information about Green
Press Initiative visit www.greenpressinitiative.org.

dedicated to

my mom,
who showed me that
creativity and good nutrition in the kitchen
make a strong family.

Contents

introduction

$W\!e$ do our bodies and the earth such a favor by eating beans. I hope you will become familiar with the various types of beans, the methods for preparing them, and the diverse range of recipes you can use to enjoy them, so that beans can be a common part of your diet.

How can we ignore one of the oldest foods known to humankind? Archeologists have unearthed fossilized lentils from periods prior to 8000 B.C. All cultures use beans in their traditional dishes. Beans are the only cultivated food plants that improve the fertility of the soil in which they are grown, through the beneficial bacteria that live on their roots and by drawing nitrogen from the air into the soil.

Eating beans has overwhelming benefits for our health. They are a rich source of protein, carbohydrates, fiber, and B vitamins and are low in fat and sodium. Beans also contain significant amounts of calcium, iron, vitamin E, phosphorus, and potassium. Research has confirmed that eating beans contributes to lowering "bad" cholesterol (LDL) and blood pressure levels, which helps prevent clogged arteries and heart disease. Beans produce a slow rise in blood sugar, which is important for people with diabetes. Studies have shown that both breast cancer and colon cancer can be controlled by hormone-like substances that are activated by digestive inhibitors in beans. Beans help in the regulation of the colon, preventing constipation and hemorrhoids.

What about the gas that so often is associated with eating beans? Humans lack the enzyme alpha-galactosidase, which is needed to digest the complex sugars in beans. When these sugars are processed in our lower intestines, gas is the result. Eating beans frequently encourages the growth of bacteria that will digest these sugars in such a way to minimize gas.

If gas is a particular problem for you, keep your portions reasonable; overeating beans is asking for trouble. If you presoak your dry beans, strain off the soaking water and discard it; then cook the beans in fresh water. This will help reduce gas. The cooking water will still make a rich bean stock. (I always save this stock and use it later in soups, bread, biscuits, or gravy.) You can add a four-inch strip of kombu, a sea vegetable that aids in digestion, to your pot of beans prior to cooking. You also can try Beano, the liquid form of alpha-galactosidase. A few drops on your first bite of beans alleviates gas. Allergy Note: Beano is made from a safe, food-grade mold; however, very rarely a sensitivity with allergic-type symptoms can occur. If this happens to you, discontinue using the product, and if you know you are galactosemic, consult your doctor before trying it. Beano also contains fish gelatin. There's a new product that's similar but completely vegetarian by Nature's Plus called "Say Yes To Beans." You can find links about it on Google by typing in (keep the quotation marks): "say yes to beans".

using beans

*M*ost of my recipes call for cooked beans, even though the cooking of the beans usually isn't listed as part of the recipe. If you're pressed for time and need to open a can, go ahead. Please be aware that many brands of canned beans have salt, sugar or corn syrup, and preservatives added, so rinse them before adding them to a recipe. Although there's a wide variety of sizes according to the manufacturer, in general, a 15-ounce or 16-ounce can yields 1½ cups cooked beans. You can check the serving size and amount of servings on the side of the can to be sure.

If you prefer frozen beans, you may use them in the same amount as canned beans. Frozen beans are not the best choice for salads; if you are using them in cooked recipes you should either thaw them out first or allow for a slightly longer cooking time.

storing dry beans

Beans are most economical if you can buy them in bulk. Store your dry beans in airtight containers in a cool, dark, dry place. I keep larger amounts of our most often used beans in their original paper bags from the store, and I have never had insects get into them.

preparing dry beans

Before soaking or cooking dry beans, check them for pieces of dirt, stones, twigs, or other foreign matter that should be removed. Rinse the beans in a colander while rubbing them with your hands to clean them. It isn't necessary to presoak beans (especially if you're going to pressure cook them), but it does cut down on the cooking time and may help digestion by reducing the sugars that cause gas. Soak beans in three times as much water as beans, either overnight or the morning before you're going to cook them for supper. You also can use the following quick-soak method. After you have checked and rinsed the beans, put them in a covered pot and bring them to a boil for one minute. Keep the pot covered and let the beans soak for one hour. This will plump the beans the same as soaking them overnight. Change the water and the beans are ready to be cooked.

open kettle cooking

If time permits, you can simmer your beans in an open kettle. Cover the beans with enough water to reach several inches above them. Bring the beans to a boil, lower the heat to a simmer, and tilt the lid to let some of the steam escape so the water won't boil over. Adding a touch of oil to the cooking water helps keep froth from forming.

pressure cooking beans

If you're not used to a pressure cooker, it may seem more trouble than it's worth. Not so! Follow the directions for the size cooker that you have; usually one cup of beans for every quart is recommended (for example, a four-quart pressure cooker will cook four cups of beans at a time). Bring it up to pressure on high heat, then turn down the heat just enough to maintain full pressure. Remember to put several drops of oil in the cooking water before you close the lid to keep the beans from creating foam, which can clog the vent of the cooker.

microwave bean cooking

Cooking beans in a microwave isn't a time saver if you're starting with dry beans. Of course, if the beans already are cooked, they can be reheated without any problem. However, I've found that using a microwave to cook dry beans doesn't decrease the cooking time significantly compared to stovetop methods.

crock-pots

Crock-Pots (also known as "slow cookers") are a convenient way to prepare beans. Before you leave the house in the morning, put a cup or two of rinsed beans into your Crock-Pot, add three times as much water, some garlic, and a bay leaf perhaps, and turn the cooker to a low setting. Your beans will be ready to use for an evening meal. Soybeans won't cook sufficiently with this method; use a pressure cooker instead.

freezing beans

Because cooking dry beans can be so time intensive, try to always cook a full pot and freeze the leftovers for future meals. Beans freeze well. Store them in pint- or quart-size containers in your freezer and they will be ready to use as soon as they thaw. Simply defrost them in the morning and they'll be ready to use for dinner. To freeze beans to put into a salad, drain the cooked beans, spread them in a single layer on a cookie sheet, and put the cookie sheet directly in the freezer. When the beans are frozen, transfer them to an airtight container or zippered freezer bag. This is a good idea for summer picnics, as the beans will help keep your cooler cold while they defrost. Bean soups and stews freeze well too, so make a full pot and freeze some for those days when you don't have time to prepare a meal.

The recommended cooking times for beans vary from one cookbook to the next, as there is quite a range of opinion on how long is long enough. Commercially canned beans are not as soft as the beans you might cook at home, but for most people, canned beans won't cause digestive problems. Since there are enough people whose systems don't do well with beans unless they are well cooked and very soft (especially children and elderly people), I recommend cooking times for beans that may seem lengthier than necessary. Cook your beans until you can easily mash them on the roof of your mouth with your tongue. You shouldn't have to chew them to get them to break up easily. The cooking times listed on the chart on page 14 will provide you with a reliable guideline for cooking various types of beans so that they are soft enough even for young children.

When referring to the cooking chart, remember that cooking times will vary depending on the age and condition of the beans. Older beans take longer to cook than fresher ones that have more moisture in them. Start timing the cooking after the water has come to a boil and been turned down to a simmer (for open kettle) or come up to pressure (for pressure cooking). Keep in mind that your altitude may affect the cooking times. At altitudes higher than sea level you may need to add several minutes to the times listed in the chart.

types of beans

From the many kinds of beans that exist, I have chosen the most available ones to use in my recipes. If you are able to find others, don't hesitate to substitute them.

ADUKI BEANS (ADZUKI) These small, reddish-brown beans are easy to digest and sweet in flavor. Aduki beans are popular in Japanese and Chinese cooking. They cook quickly, so watch closely to prevent them from getting mushy. If you cook them with rice, they turn the rice a pretty shade of pink. You may have to go to an Asian or natural food store to find these beans.

ANASAZI BEANS The ancestor of pinto beans, these lovely purple- and white-flecked beans have a rich flavor. Anasazi means "ancient ones" in the Navaho language. Anasazi beans cook faster than pintos and go well in Mexican dishes with chili peppers, garlic, and cumin.

BLACK BEANS (TURTLE) Black beans are a staple of Cuban, Latin American, and Asian diets. They are low in fat and are a good match with corn and rice. Consider using coriander and lime juice for spicing up your black beans.

BLACK-EYED PEAS (COWPEAS) These thin-skinned peas are popular in recipes from India, Africa, and southeastern United States. They cook quickly and make great stuffings, casseroles, and soups. Black-eyed peas have a distinct, nutty flavor and are low in fat and high in iron.

GARBANZO BEANS (CHICKPEAS) You'll find these round, beige beans in dishes from the Mediterranean and India. They are a good source of calcium and have the highest fat content of all beans except soybeans. Their nutty flavor makes them very versatile. Try them in dips, soup, salads, curries, or burgers.

GREAT NORTHERN BEANS See white beans.

KIDNEY BEANS Kidney beans have a distinct, rich flavor, a firm texture, and are a good source of iron and potassium. They make the best chili and also are good in salads, soups, and casseroles.

LENTILS (PULSES, DAL) Lentils, derived from the Latin "lens," are perhaps the oldest legume of our civilization. There are many kinds of lentils; green, brown, and orange are the ones most commonly found in the U.S. Lentils are easy to sprout. They cook quickly, have a creamy texture, and are great in curry dishes.

LIMA BEANS (BABY LIMAS AND BUTTER BEANS) Lima beans originated in South America. A starchy bean, they have more potassium and vitamin C than any other legume. When soaked, limas cook quickly. Watch them carefully if you want them to keep their shape or if you plan to use them in a salad.

NAVY BEANS See white beans.

PINTO BEANS The popular pinto bean is plump, with pinkish brown flecks and an earthy flavor that blends so well with Mexican spices: garlic, chilies, and cumin. Pinto cultivation is abundant in southwest Colorado, although the beans are native to Mexico.

SOYBEANS From central China we get the nutritious and versatile soybean. It contains all of the essential amino acids plus lecithin and has the highest fat content of any legume. The list of soy-based foods is impressive: tofu, tempeh, tamari, textured vegetable protein, soy oil, soy flour and grits, soy milk, soy ice cream, soy yogurt, soy nuts, soy butter, and miso, as well as many meat substitutes. Because it takes so long to get soybeans really soft by cooking them in an open kettle, I strongly recommend using a pressure cooker. Be sure to add a teaspoon of oil to the pressure cooker before cooking soybeans. They tend to foam and their hulls will clog the vent. Listen closely to the pressure cooker when cooking—if the steady sizzle of steam is interrupted you should turn off the heat, bring down the pressure, and check to see if the vent is clogged. Cleaning up a pressure cooker explosion is no fun.

SPLIT PEAS Besides the common green split pea, you'll also find the yellow variety, which has a milder flavor. Perfect for soups and dips, split peas are a good source of vitamin A and are very low in fat. It's not necessary to presoak split peas. They take a little over an hour to cook in an open kettle.

WHITE BEANS (NAVY, GREAT NORTHERN, CANNELLINI) We are familiar with these in baked beans, but they're also great for soups and stews. They don't take long to cook. Compared with other beans, they're high in fiber, calcium, and vitamin E. The mild flavor of these beans goes well with thyme, savory, or rosemary.

*Bean Cooking Chart*_____

Use three cups of water for each cup of dry beans.

	Soaked, open-kettle	No soak and pressure cook	Soak and pressure cook	Yield per 2 cups dry
aduki	30 min	15 min	5-10 min	6⅔
Anasazi	60 min	25 min	15 min	5
black	90 min	30-35 min	20 min	5
black-eyed peas	25 min	10 min	5-8 min	4¾
garbanzo	4 hr. 25 min	35 min	25 min	5
Great Northern	90 min	25 min	20 min	5
kidney	35-40 min	30 min	15-20 min	4½
lentil, brown*	20-25 min	**	**	5
lentil, orange*	15-20 min	**	**	3⅓
lima, baby	30 min	10-15 min	8 min	4
navy	35-40 min	22 min	15 min	5
pinto	90 min	35-40 min	20-25 min	5
soybeans	**	60 min	45 min	4
split peas*	75-90 min	7 min	**	4

*It is not necessary to presoak lentils and split peas.

**Do not use this method for this variety of beans.

more
fabulous
beans

recipes

dips and spreads

These dips will keep at least a week in the refrigerator if your beans are fresh. Most dips are tasty when they are first made, but their flavors develop more as they sit chilled.

dark star
pinto dip

My son, a Grateful Dead fan, created this recipe and consumes massive quantities of it when we have taco salad for dinner.

Combine in a food processor:

    3 cups cooked pinto beans
    ½ cup chopped tomatoes
    ½ cup spaghetti sauce
    ½ cup mild or hot salsa
    ⅓ cup chopped onions
    ⅓ cup chopped green bell peppers
    1 jalapeño pepper, seeded and chopped
    ½ teaspoon salt (optional)

Blend until somewhat chunky. Serve immediately or thoroughly chilled.

yields 4 cups

per ¼ cup:

calories 52
protein 3 g
fat 0 g
carb 10 g
fiber 3 g
sodium 93 mg

gremolata

Preheat the oven to 350°F. Peel:

    10 cloves garlic

Place on a baking sheet and roast in the oven for 10 minutes.

Combine the roasted garlic in a blender with:

    2 cups cooked white beans (navy or lima)
    ¼ cup fresh lemon juice
    ¼ cup chopped fresh parsley
    ½ teaspoon salt (optional)
    ¼ teaspoon pepper

Process until smooth. Add a little bean stock or water if the dip is too thick.

This tasty dip can be served with raw carrots and bell peppers or on crackers or rice cakes.

yields 2 cups

per ¼ cup:

calories 73
protein 4 g
fat 0 g
carb 14 g
fiber 3 g
sodium 2 mg

barbecue black *bean dip*

In a small skillet, sauté until beginning to brown:

   ¾ cup chopped onions
   ½ teaspoon canola oil

Transfer to a food processor and add:

   2 cups cooked black beans
   ¼ cup apple cider vinegar
   ¼ cup tomato paste
   2 to 3 tablespoons honey or brown sugar
   1 tablespoon vegetarian Worcestershire sauce
   1 tablespoon spicy mustard
   ½ teaspoon ground allspice
   Salt to taste

Process until very smooth. Serve immediately or chilled along with corn chips or celery sticks.

yields 2¼ cups

per ¼ cup:

calories 81
protein 4 g
fat 1 g
carb 16 g
fiber 4 g
sodium 58 mg

golden yellow
split pea dip

Combine in a medium saucepan:

> 3 cups water
> 1 cup dry yellow split peas

Bring to a boil, reduce the heat, cover, and simmer, stirring occasionally, for 1¼ hours or until the peas are quite soft. Remove from the heat and let stand, covered, until cool. Drain any excess liquid.

Combine in a food processor:

> 2 tablespoons frozen orange juice concentrate
> 2 tablespoons white miso
> 2 tablespoons nutritional yeast flakes
> 1 tablespoon minced garlic (about 2 cloves)
> ½ teaspoon paprika

Purée until smooth and stir into the cooked split peas. Serve warm or thoroughly chilled.

yields 2 cups

per ¼ cup:

calories 81
protein 6 g
fat 1 g
carb 14 g
fiber 4 g
sodium 104 mg

garbanzo
spread

Enjoy this spread with a chunk of Italian or dark rye bread.

In a medium skillet, sauté until soft:

> 1 clove garlic, chopped
> ½ cup chopped onions
> ½ teaspoon olive oil

Stir in and sauté just until the parsley has wilted:

> ½ cup chopped fresh parsley
> 1 tablespoon chopped fresh basil, or 1 teaspoon dried basil
> 1 teaspoon chopped fresh oregano, or ½ teaspoon dried oregano

Combine in a food processor with:

> 3 cups cooked garbanzo beans
> ½ cup bean stock or water
> 2 tablespoons fresh lemon juice
> ½ teaspoon salt (optional)
> ¼ teaspoon ground cumin

Process until smooth. Alternatively, transfer the onions and herbs to a bowl. Mash the beans, add the remaining ingredients, and mix well with a fork.

yields 3½ cups

per ¼ cup:

calories 63
protein 3 g
fat 0 g
carb 10 g
fiber 2 g
sodium 4 mg

west indies pinto
or kidney bean dip

Here's a spicy dip that is perfect to serve with corn chips as an appetizer or party snack.

Combine in a food processor:

2½ cups cooked pinto or kidney beans

⅔ cup chopped tomatoes

¼ cup finely chopped onions

¼ cup bean stock or water

2 tablespoons fresh lemon or lime juice

1 tablespoon tamari

2 cloves garlic, minced

1 teaspoon ground coriander

1 teaspoon ground cumin

½ teaspoon curry powder

½ teaspoon dried oregano

½ teaspoon chili powder

Process until smooth. Alternatively, mash the beans with a fork, add the remaining ingredients, and mix until well combined. Chill thoroughly before serving. This is good to serve with corn chips.

yields 2⅔ cups

per ¼ cup:

calories 58

protein 3 g

fat 0 g

carb 11 g

fiber 4 g

sodium 93 mg

garbanzo bean
hummus

This rich spread is a terrific match with pita bread, sprouts, and tomatoes. We like it as a travel food to put in our cooler when we can't prepare a meal.

Combine in a blender or food processor:

2 cups cooked garbanzo beans
¼ cup bean stock or water
¼ cup fresh lemon juice
3 tablespoons tahini
2 tablespoons chopped fresh parsley
1 tablespoon tamari
2 cloves garlic, chopped

Purée until smooth. Chill in the refrigerator for at least 30 minutes before serving to allow the flavors to develop.

yields 2 cups

per ¼ cup:

calories 104
protein 5 g
fat 4 g
carb 14 g
fiber 3 g
sodium 133 mg

variation: hummus eggplant dip

Preheat the oven to 350°F. Place on a baking sheet or in a small pan:

1 small eggplant

Bake for 20 to 30 minutes or until the eggplant is soft in the middle. Scoop out the flesh and mash well. Purée along with the hummus or stir it into the finished dip.

yields 2¾ cups

per ¼ cup:

calories 89
protein 4 g
fat 3 g
carb 13 g
fiber 3 g
sodium 98 mg

carrot garbanzo
dip

Combine in a medium saucepan:

2 cups chopped carrots

1 cup bean stock or water

⅔ cup chopped onions

2 cloves garlic, coarsely chopped

Bring to a boil, reduce the heat, and simmer for 10 to15 minutes or until the carrots and onions are tender. Combine in a food processor with:

1½ cups cooked garbanzo beans

2 tablespoons fresh lemon juice

2 teaspoons dried mint

½ teaspoon salt (optional)

Blend until smooth. Serve immediately or chilled along with toasted pita bread pieces, rice cakes, or raw bell pepper and celery sticks.

yields 3 cups

per ¼ cup:

calories 50

protein 2 g

fat 1 g

carb 9 g

fiber 2 g

sodium 19 mg

lentil
pâté

This may be thinly sliced to serve with crackers, or you can keep it in a block to use as a dip or spread.

Preheat the oven to 350°F. Lightly oil a bread pan and set aside.

Combine in a medium saucepan:

    3 cups water
    1 cup dry lentils

Bring to a boil, reduce the heat, cover, and cook for 30 to 35 minutes.

Tear or chop into chunks:

    2 cups sourdough bread

Place in a medium bowl. When the lentils have finished cooking, drain any extra cooking water into a measuring cup. Press the lentils with the back of a slotted spoon to allow the extra stock to flow into the cup. Add enough water to make 1 cup of liquid, and pour it over the sourdough bread pieces. Stir to soften all of the bread.

In a small skillet, sauté until soft:

    1 cup chopped onions
    1 cup chopped celery (about 3 stalks)
    1 teaspoon olive oil

yields 3 cups

per ¼ cup:

calories 78
protein 5 g
fat 1 g
carb 13 g
fiber 4 g
sodium 228 mg

Transfer to a food process along with the drained lentils, soaked bread, and:

    2 tablespoons tamari
    1 teaspoon dried tarragon
    1 teaspoon dried thyme
    ¼ teaspoon ground cloves
    ⅛ teaspoon pepper

Process until well blended. Pour into the prepared bread pan and bake for 40 minutes. Cool and refrigerate overnight. The pâté will slip out of the pan when it is turned over onto a serving plate.

white bean
spread

Enjoy this flavorful spread with pita bread, crackers, or raw vegetables.

Drain and mash:

    2 cups cooked white beans (navy or lima)

While the beans are hot, add:

    ½ cup finely chopped tomatoes
    ¼ cup minced red onions
    ½ teaspoon ground cumin
    ¼ teaspoon salt
    ⅛ teaspoon pepper
    juice of 1 lemon

Mix well. Serve warm or cold.

yields 2¼ cups

per ¼ cup:

calories 62
protein 4 g
fat 0 g
carb 12 g
fiber 2 g
sodium 61 mg

soy
nuts

These crunchy, roasted beans are a great snack. They are high in protein but not as high in fat as regular nuts. Take them with you hiking, or have them on hand for afternoon snacks.

In a large pot, soak overnight:

    4 cups water
    2 cups dry soybeans

The next morning, drain the soak water, and add enough fresh water to cover the beans by one inch. Bring to a boil for 5 minutes, and remove any hulls that float to the top. Cover the pot and let stand for one hour or longer.

Preheat the oven to 350°F. Lightly oil a cookie sheet. Drain the beans and pour them onto the cookie sheet, spreading them in a single layer. Bake for 35 to 45 minutes or until lightly browned. Shake the pan or stir the beans with a wide spoon or spatula a few times during baking. Remove from the oven and sprinkle with salt. Let cool completely; then transfer to an airtight container. Store at room temperature. These will stay fresh for several months.

yields 3 cups

per ¼ cup:

calories 74
protein 7 g
fat 4 g
carb 4 g
fiber 3 g
sodium 0 mg

chickpea
nuts

yields 3 cups

per ¼ cup:

calories 67
protein 4 g
fat 1 g
carb 11 g
fiber 2 g
sodium 3 mg

Prepare as for Soy Nuts, but use garbanzo beans instead of soybeans. For Spiced Chickpea Nuts, sprinkle the beans with tamari and garlic powder before baking.

salads and seasonings

tropical black bean
salad

Thanks to my mother-in-law, Rose, who gave me the idea for this recipe. Although this combination of ingredients is a bit unusual, it makes an exquisite and unique salad or entrée. Try serving it with fresh corn bread or a dark loaf of pumpernickel.

Combine in a medium serving bowl:

3 cups cooled, cooked black beans

2 cups cubed mangos (2 to 3 fruits)

2 cups chopped fresh pineapple

½ cup chopped onions

3 tablespoons fresh lime juice

3 cloves garlic, minced

1 jalapeño pepper, seeded and minced

½ teaspoon salt (optional)

Stir gently until well combined. Serve at once or marinate in the refrigerator overnight to allow the flavors to blend.

yields 6 servings

per serving:

calories 195

protein 9 g

fat 1 g

carb 41 g

fiber 10 g

sodium 106 mg

white bean
salad

Combine in a large bowl:

  3½ cups drained, cooked white beans
  ½ cup chopped fresh parsley
  ½ cup chopped black olives (optional)
  ¼ cup chopped fresh mint, or 1 teaspoon dried mint
  ¼ cup fresh lemon juice
  6 to 8 scallions, chopped
  1 tablespoon olive oil
  1 tablespoon apple cider or juice
  3 cloves garlic, minced
  1 teaspoon salt (optional)
  ¼ teaspoon dried thyme
  ¼ teaspoon dried tarragon
  ¼ teaspoon pepper

Toss gently until evenly combined. Refrigerate for several hours before serving or overnight to allow the full flavor to develop.

yields 4 to 6 servings

per serving:

calories 215
protein 13 g
fat 3 g
carb 35 g
fiber 9 g
sodium 15 mg

kidney bean
and sprouted lentil salad

To prepare the dressing, combine in small jar with a tight fitting lid:

¼ cup apple cider

3 tablespoons balsamic vinegar

2 tablespoons tamari

2 tablespoons minced fresh dill weed, or 1 teaspoon dried dill weed

1 tablespoon olive oil

½ teaspoon paprika

¼ teaspoon pepper

Shake vigorously until well blended.

Combine in a salad bowl:

1½ cups cooked kidney beans

1½ cups cooked green beans

1½ cups cooked white or brown rice

1 cup chopped celery

1 cup chopped bell peppers

¾ cup sprouted lentils (see page 50)

⅔ cup sliced red onions

Pour the dressing over all, and toss gently until well combined. If time permits, chill the salad before serving to allow the flavors to develop.

yields 6 servings

per serving:

calories 169

protein 8 g

fat 3 g

carb 30 g

fiber 6 g

sodium 359 mg

carrot and garbanzo
salad

Prepare this salad several hours before serving so it can marinate and allow the full flavor to develop.

Combine in a medium serving bowl:

    2 cups cooked garbanzo beans
    1 cup grated carrots
    1 cup grated cucumbers
    ¼ cup minced fresh parsley
    2 scallions, finely chopped
    1 clove garlic, pressed

To make the dressing, combine in a small jar with a tight fitting lid:

    2 tablespoons tahini
    1 tablespoon water or apple juice
    1 tablespoon balsamic vinegar
    1 teaspoon tamari

Shake vigorously until well blended. Pour the dressing over the salad, toss gently, and refrigerate a few hours before serving, if time permits, to allow the flavors to blend. Toss the salad a few times while it chills.

yields 4 to 6 servings

per serving:

calories 163
protein 8 g
fat 5 g
carb 24 g
fiber 6 g
sodium 87 mg

lima gazpacho
salad

The flavor of this salad improves if it is made in advance and allowed to marinate for a few hours before serving. It makes a wonderful accompaniment to a picnic or cook-out.

Combine in a medium bowl:

   2 cups chopped fresh tomatoes
   1 cucumber, chopped
   1 green bell pepper, chopped
   1 avocado, chopped
   5 scallions, chopped
   2 cloves garlic, minced

Gently stir in:

   2 cups cooked lima beans or butter beans

To make the dressing, combine in a small jar with a tight fitting lid:

   ¼ cup balsamic vinegar
   1 tablespoon olive oil
   ¼ teaspoon dried basil
   ¼ teaspoon dried oregano
   Salt and pepper to taste

Shake vigorously until well blended. Pour the dressing over the salad, toss gently but thoroughly, and chill until ready to serve.

yields 6 servings

per serving:

calories 179
protein 7 g
fat 8 g
carb 23 g
fiber 8 g
sodium 14 mg

tabouli
with garbanzos

The addition of garbanzo beans to this traditional dish makes it a complete meal.

Combine in a small saucepan and bring to a boil:

2 cups water

Remove the pan from the heat, and stir in:

1 cup bulgur

Mix well and cover tightly. Let stand for 30 minutes. Allow the bulgur to cool completely; then transfer it to a salad bowl.

To prepare the dressing, combine in a blender:

½ cup fresh peppermint
⅓ cup fresh lemon juice
2 tablespoons olive oil
2 tablespoons tamari
2 cloves garlic, chopped
¼ teaspoon pepper

Add to the cooled bulgur in the salad bowl:

1½ cups cooked garbanzo beans
2 large tomatoes, chopped
1 cucumber, chopped
1 cup chopped fresh parsley
½ cup chopped scallions
½ cup pitted and halved ripe olives (optional)

Pour the dressing over the salad, toss well, and chill for several hours before serving.

yields 6 servings

per serving:

calories 181
protein 7 g
fat 6 g
carb 28 g
fiber 6 g
sodium 346 mg

lentil-lime
salad

Combine in a medium saucepan:

> 5 cups water
> 1½ cups lentils
> 1 bay leaf
> 1 clove garlic, cut into chunks

Bring to a boil, reduce the heat, cover, and cook 25 to 30 minutes or until the lentils are soft. Remove the bay leaf and garlic, drain, and cool.

In a medium serving bowl, combine the drained lentils with:

> ½ cup chopped celery
> ¼ cup minced fresh parsley
> 3 scallions, finely chopped
> ½ fresh chili pepper, seeded and minced

To prepare the dressing, combine in a small jar with a tight fitting lid:

> 3 tablespoons fresh lime juice
> 1½ tablespoons tamari
> 1 tablespoon balsamic vinegar
> 1 tablespoon olive oil
> 2 cloves garlic, minced or pressed
> ½ teaspoon grated lime peel
> ½ teaspoon ground cumin

Shake vigorously until well blended. Pour the dressing over the lentil and vegetable mixture, toss gently, and refrigerate for at least one hour to enhance the flavors.

*yields 4 to 6
servings*

per serving:

calories 175
protein 12 g
fat 3 g
carb 27 g
fiber 10 g
sodium 321 mg

pineapple-lentil
salad

Heat in a medium skillet:

> 1 teaspoon olive oil

When hot, add:

> 2 teaspoons grated fresh gingerroot
> 1 teaspoon ground cumin
> ½ teaspoon ground coriander

Stir constantly until the spices begin to release a pleasant aroma, about 1 minute. Then stir in:

> 2½ cups drained, cooked lentils

Mix well, remove from the heat, and cool.

Transfer the lentils to a serving bowl. Add:

> 1 (20-ounce) can unsweetened pineapple chunks (reserve the juice)
> 2 large tomatoes, chopped

To prepare the dressing, combine in a small jar with a tight fitting lid:

> ⅓ cup pineapple juice (reserved from the chunks)
> 2 tablespoons apple cider vinegar
> 1 tablespoon tamari
> 1 teaspoon spicy mustard
> 1 clove garlic, minced or pressed

Shake vigorously until well blended. Pour the dressing over the salad and toss well. Chill before serving.

yields 6 servings

per serving:

calories 171
protein 9 g
fat 1 g
carb 34 g
fiber 7 g
sodium 182 mg

kidney bean *salad*

Basmati rice is a nice complement to the Indian spices in this delicious salad.

Combine in a serving bowl:

> 2 cups cooked kidney beans
>
> 2 cups cooked brown, white, or basmati rice
>
> 3 scallions, chopped
>
> 1 green or red bell pepper, chopped
>
> ⅓ cup chopped walnuts
>
> ⅓ cup raisins

To prepare the dressing, combine in a blender:

> 3 to 4 tablespoons fresh lemon juice
>
> 1 cup plain nondairy yogurt
>
> 1 tablespoon maple syrup or sweetener of your choice
>
> 1 teaspoon ground coriander
>
> 1 teaspoon ground cumin
>
> ½ teaspoon turmeric
>
> ½ teaspoon Garam Masala (page 49)
>
> ½ teaspoon salt (optional)
>
> 1 clove garlic

Pour the dressing over the salad, and toss until well combined.

yields 6 servings

per serving:

calories 240

protein 9 g

fat 6 g

carb 41 g

fiber 7 g

sodium 14 mg

more fabulous beans

spinach salad
with garbanzos

Fresh and crispy, this salad is as tasty as they come.

Combine in a serving bowl:

> 6 cups coarsely chopped fresh spinach leaves
>
> 2 cups sliced mushrooms
>
> 1½ cups slivered sunchokes (Jerusalem artichokes)
>
> 1½ cups cooked garbanzo beans
>
> 1 cup grated carrots
>
> 1 cup thinly sliced red onion crescents

Sprinkle over the mixture:

> 3 tablespoons fresh lime juice
>
> 2 tablespoons toasted sesame seeds
>
> 2 tablespoons olive oil
>
> 1 tablespoon tamari
>
> 3 cloves garlic, minced

Toss gently but thoroughly. Serve immediately or let marinate for 30 minutes at room temperature or for a few hours in the refrigerator so the flavors can marry.

yields 6 servings

per serving:

calories 188

protein 8 g

fat 7 g

carb 25 g

fiber 6 g

sodium 224 mg

pinto bean
taco salad

This is a fun meal because everyone gets to make unique combinations to suit their individual tastes. Amounts to have on hand will vary depending on the appetites of those at the table.

Have ready:

 5 cups baked corn chips (one 12-ounce bag)
 2½ cups cooked pinto beans, mashed,
  or 2 to 3 cups Dark Star Pinto Dip (see page 18)

TOPPINGS:

 2 cups finely chopped lettuce, or alfalfa sprouts
 1 cucumber, chopped
 1 onion, chopped
 1 green pepper, chopped
 1 carrot, grated
 1 tomato, chopped
 1 avocado, thinly sliced (optional)

CONDIMENTS:

 hot salsa
 ketchup
 mayonnaise
 mustard
 nutritional yeast

To assemble, crush a handful of corn chips on a plate, spoon some mashed beans or bean dip on top of them, and sprinkle on any or all of the toppings, followed by the condiments of your choice. Serve at once.

yields 5 servings

per serving:

 calories 265
 protein 12 g
 fat 2 g
 carb 54 g
 fiber 12 g
 sodium 156 mg

thai-inspired
white bean salad

A tangy dressing brings this interesting combination of beans alive.

Have ready:

> 2 cups cooked white beans or lima beans

Steam until crisp-tender, about 3 to 5 minutes:

> 3 cups diagonally cut green beans

Rinse under cold water to cool.

Drain both beans and set aside.

To prepare the dressing, combine in a jar with a tight fitting lid:

> ½ cup fresh lime juice
> ½ cup minced fresh mint leaves
> 2 tablespoons tamari
> 1 tablespoon sugar
> 2 cloves garlic, minced
> 1 fresh chili or jalapeño pepper, seeded and minced
> ¼ teaspoon salt (optional)

Shake until well blended. Combine the green beans and drained white beans in a serving bowl, and pour the dressing over them. Toss gently until evenly coated with the dressing, taking care that the beans stay whole. Refrigerate at least one hour before serving.

yields 6 servings

per serving:

calories 117
protein 8 g
fat 0 g
carb 23 g
fiber 6 g
sodium 342 mg

crunchy asian
soybean salad

This salad is wonderful served fresh, but the flavors really pop if you marinate it overnight.

To prepare the dressing, combine in a small jar with a tight fitting lid:

    3 tablespoons rice vinegar
    2 tablespoons tamari
    1½ tablespoons dark sesame oil
    1 tablespoon brown sugar
    1 tablespoon ketchup
    1 clove garlic, minced

Shake vigorously until well blended. Set aside.

Steam for 3 minutes or until tender-crisp:

    3 cups bite-size broccoli florets
    2 cups fresh or frozen snow peas

If you use frozen snow peas, add them after 2 minutes and steam them with the broccoli for 2 minutes. Rinse under cold water to rapidly cool the vegetables. Transfer to a serving bowl and add:

    2 cups very thinly sliced Napa cabbage
    16 ounces baby corn
    1½ cups cooked soybeans
    1 red bell pepper, chopped
    5 ounces bamboo shoots
    5 mushrooms, sliced
    4 scallions, chopped

yields 6 servings

per serving:
calories 186
protein 13 g
fat 8 g
carb 20 g
fiber 8 g
sodium 435 mg

Pour the dressing over the vegetables and toss gently. Cover and let rest at room temperature up to 30 minutes or in the refrigerator for a few hours before serving, tossing occasionally.

more fabulous beans

soybeans
and sprouts salad

Combine in a medium salad bowl:

    2 cups cooked soybeans
    2 cups finely chopped Chinese cabbage
    1 cup mung bean sprouts (see page 50)
    2 carrots, shredded
    2 stalks celery, finely chopped
    1 bunch scallions, chopped
    ½ cup sliced water chestnuts
    1 tablespoon toasted sesame seeds

To prepare the dressing, combine in a small jar with a tight fitting lid:

    ¼ cup apple juice
    2 tablespoons balsamic vinegar
    1½ tablespoons tamari
    1 tablespoon olive oil
    1 tablespoon grated fresh gingerroot
    1 chili pepper, seeded and minced
    1 clove garlic, minced

Shake vigorously until well blended. Pour over the beans vegetables and toss gently. Serve at once or chill for a few hours in the refrigerator.

yields 6 servings

per serving:

calories 168
protein 12 g
fat 8 g
carb 15 g
fiber 6 g
sodium 293 mg

edamame gado gado
salad

Enjoy this Indonesian salad that uses edamame, which are green soybeans. They commonly are found in the frozen food section of natural food stores and some supermarkets. Because the beans often are still in their pods, it takes a little time to squeeze them out, but this is part of the fun of using them.

Have ready:

    1 head bibb lettuce, washed and trimmed
    2 cups fresh pineapple chunks, or 1 (20-ounce) can
    1½ cups mung bean sprouts (see page 50)
    2 tomatoes, cut into wedges
    1 cucumber, seeded and thinly sliced lengthwise

Fill a medium saucepan partway with water and add:

    2 cups boiled, peeled, and cubed sweet potatoes

Bring to a boil, reduce the heat, and simmer until tender. Drain, cool, and set aside.

Fill a medium saucepan partway with water and add:

    1 cup edamame

Bring to a boil, reduce the heat, and simmer for 3 to 5 minutes.

Cool and squeeze the beans out of their pods. Set aside.

To prepare the dressing, combine in a small jar with a tight fitting lid:

    ¼ cup fresh lime juice
    2 tablespoons smooth peanut butter
    1½ tablespoons coconut milk
    2 tablespoons tamari
    1 tablespoon brown sugar
    3 cloves garlic, minced
    ¼ teaspoon dried red pepper flakes

Shake vigorously to make a smooth dressing.

yields 5 servings

per serving:

calories 242
protein 10 g
fat 7 g
carb 39 g
fiber 7 g
sodium 338 mg

Arrange the lettuce leaves on 4 individual salad plates. On top of each bed of lettuce, place the pineapple chunks, mung bean sprouts, tomato wedges, cucumber slices, sweet potatoes, and edamame. Drizzle the dressing evenly over each of the salads and serve.

sweet 'n sour cabbage
and kidney salad

Steam for 3 minutes:

> 1 cup chopped broccoli

Rinse immediately under cold water to cool. Drain well and transfer to a salad bowl Add:

> 2 cups cooked kidney beans
> 1 cucumber, thinly sliced
> 1 cup shredded cabbage
> ½ cup chopped celery

To prepare the dressing, combine in a small jar with a tight fitting lid:

> 2 tablespoons tamari
> 3 tablespoons apple cider vinegar
> 1 tablespoon olive oil
> 1 tablespoon liquid sweetener of your choice
> 1 clove garlic, minced

yields 6 servings

per serving:

calories 114
protein 7 g
fat 3 g
carb 17 g
fiber 5 g
sodium 352 mg

Shake vigorously until well blended. Pour the dressing over the salad, toss until well combined, and refrigerate for several hours before serving, tossing occasionally.

garbanzo and olive
pasta salad

Combine in a salad bowl:

3½ cups cooked pasta spirals (2 cups dry)
2½ cups cooked garbanzo beans
1½ cups chopped celery
1 cup salad olives
¾ cup chopped scallions

To prepare the dressing, combine in a blender in a jar with a tight fitting lid:

¼ cup balsamic vinegar
¼ cup water or apple cider
1 tablespoon olive oil
1 tablespoon tamari
1 tablespoon maple syrup or sweetener of your choice
1 teaspoon spicy mustard
½ teaspoon paprika

Blend or shake vigorously until well mixed. Pour the dressing over the pasta, and toss until evenly combined. Serve at once or refrigerate, stirring occasionally, until ready to serve.

yields 6 servings

per serving:

calories 273
protein 11 g
fat 6 g
carb 46 g
fiber 6 g
sodium 417 mg

mexican black bean
salad

Enjoy the cilantro or substitute parsley if you prefer. This salad makes a handy lunch and leftovers are equally delicious the next day.

In a medium saucepan, cook in boiling water until nearly tender:

2 cups peeled and diced potatoes

Add and cook for 2 to 3 more minutes:

1 cup chopped carrots

Add:

1 cup frozen corn

Stir and drain. Rinse under cold water to quickly cool the vegetables and stop the cooking process. Drain well.

Combine in a medium serving bowl:

1½ cups cooked black beans
1 red bell pepper, chopped

6 radishes, thinly sliced
5 scallions, chopped

Add the potatoes, carrots, and corn.

Combine in medium bowl:

¾ cup medium-hot salsa
½ cup chopped fresh cilantro or parsley
½ cup low-sodium tomato juice
2 tablespoons fresh lime juice
1 tablespoon olive oil

Mix well and pour over the vegetables. Toss gently but thoroughly. Before serving, top with:

1 avocado, chopped into bite-size pieces

yields 6 servings

per serving:

calories 227
protein 7 g
fat 8 g
carb 35 g
fiber 9 g
sodium 145 mg

potato pinto
salad

Here is a hearty, summer picnic salad, even if the picnic is just out on the deck.

In a medium saucepan, cook in boiling water until almost tender:

> 2 cups peeled and diced potatoes

Add:

> 10 ounces frozen peas

Return to a boil and cook until the potatoes are tender. Drain well.

To make the dressing, combine in a small jar with a tight fitting lid:

> 1 cup plain nondairy yogurt
> 3 tablespoons apple cider vinegar
> 1 tablespoon spicy mustard
> ¼ teaspoon pepper
> Salt to taste

Shake vigorously until well blended. Set aside.

Combine in a serving bowl:

> 1½ cups cooked pinto beans
> 1 cup chopped celery
> 1 cup sliced ripe olives
> ½ cup minced red onions
> ½ cup chopped fresh dill weed

Pour the dressing over vegetables and beans and toss until they are evenly coated. Add the potatoes and peas, and carefully toss again until evenly combined. Serve at once or chill for several hours in the refrigerator to allow the flavors to blend.

yields 5 servings

per serving:
calories 245
protein 10 g
fat 6 g
carb 39 g
fiber 10 g
sodium 256 mg

garam

masala

Here is a sweet and spicy blend of ground spices that lends a distinctive taste to dishes like Curried Garbanzos (page 109) and Masoor Dal (page 112). Use it to experiment with other vegetable and bean dishes.

Combine in a small jar with a tight fitting lid:

- 4 teaspoons ground coriander
- 2 teaspoons ground cumin
- 1 teaspoon pepper
- 1 teaspoon ground cloves
- 1 teaspoon ground cinnamon
- 1 teaspoon ground cardamom

Shake well to mix thoroughly. Label the jar and store it with your spices until ready to use.

yields 3⅓ tablespoons

sprouted *beans*

Sprouted beans are a healthful and tasty addition to fresh dishes like Edamame Gado Gado Salad (pages 44-45) and Crunchy Asian Soybean Salad (page 42). Toss them onto sandwiches and wraps, and use them in stir-fry dishes like Bean Sprout Curry (page 148). The sprouting process can be as simple or as complicated as you choose; there are all kinds of sprouting jars, bags, and books on the subject. This super easy method works well with mung beans and lentils, as well as larger beans such as garbanzo.

Soak overnight in a wide-mouth glass jar:

   3 cups water
   ½ to 1 cup dry beans

The next morning, drain all the water and cover the jar with a piece of cheesecloth secured with a rubber band. Put the jar on its side and rinse and drain the beans twice a day. The sprouts should be ready in 4 to 5 days. Many sprouts will grow several inches long. If you aren't going to eat the sprouts right away, put them in the refrigerator so they will stay fresh. They will keep for about a week depending on the particular bean.

soups and chowders

great northern
mushroom soup

This creamy soup with chunks of vegetables is mellow and soothing, perfect for a weekend lunch. Look for unusual mushrooms to vary the flavor of this soup from time to time.

If you are starting with dry beans, combine in a 3-quart soup pot:

4 cups water
1 cup dry Great Northern beans

Bring to a boil, reduce the heat, cover, and cook until soft, about 1¼ hours.

If using canned or precooked beans, have ready:

2½ cups canned or cooked Great Northern beans

In a medium skillet, sauté until soft:

2 cups sliced mushrooms
1 medium onion, chopped
½ cup diced carrots

1 clove garlic, minced
½ teaspoon olive oil

In a blender or food processor, blend the beans with:

3 cups bean stock, veggie broth, or water

Pour the blended beans into the soup pot, and add:

¼ teaspoon dried marjoram
¼ teaspoon dried thyme
¼ teaspoon dried savory

⅛ teaspoon black or white
pepper
salt to taste

Add the sautéed vegetables and bring to a slow boil. Lower the heat and simmer for 5 minutes.

yields 4 servings

per serving:

calories 166
protein 11 g
fat 1 g
carb 30 g
fiber 9 g
sodium 11 mg

spicy golden
split pea soup

This spicy soup is excellent served with a chunk of bread for dipping. You can vary the amount of garam masala to make it as hot or as mild as you like.

Heat in a 3-quart soup pot:

> 1 teaspoon canola oil

When hot, add and sauté until soft

> 1 onion, chopped
> 2 cloves garlic, minced

Stir in:

> 1 teaspoon ground coriander
> 1 teaspoon turmeric
> ½ teaspoon Garam Masala (page 49)
> ¼ teaspoon dried red pepper flakes

Sauté for several minutes. Then add:

> 6 cups water
> 1½ cups dry yellow split peas

Bring to a boil, reduce the heat, partially cover, and simmer for 1½ hours or until the peas begin to lose their form. Just before serving, season with:

> 1 tablespoon fresh lime juice
> ½ teaspoon salt (optional)

yields 4 to 6 servings

per serving:

calories 162
protein 10 g
fat 1 g
carb 28 g
fiber 10 g
sodium 4 mg

soups and chowders　　　　　**53**

autumn white
bean soup

This soup can be made quickly with precooked or canned beans, or you can start with one cup of dry beans, cook them for one hour in vegetable stock or water, and then proceed with the directions.

In a 3-quart soup pot, bring to a boil:

> 5 cups vegetable stock or water

Add:

> 1 cup finely chopped turnips
> ⅓ cup millet
> ¼ cup finely chopped scallions (about 5)
> 2 cloves garlic, minced

Cover and cook for 15 minutes.

Stir in:

> 2 cups cooked white beans (navy or Great Northern)
> 1 cup chopped fresh, frozen, or canned green beans
> ½ cup sliced mushrooms
> ¼ cup chopped fresh parsley
> 1 tablespoon tamari
> ½ teaspoon dried tarragon
> ¼ teaspoon dried rosemary

Cover and continue to cook for 10 minutes. Remove from the heat and let rest, covered, for 5 minutes before serving. Add more water if the soup is too thick.

yields 4 servings

per serving:

calories 212
protein 11 g
fat 1 g
carb 41 g
fiber 8 g
sodium 280 mg

more fabulous beans

african green
split pea soup

Be ready for a special treat when you embellish the plain split pea with this array of exotic spices.

Tie in a piece of cheesecloth (so it can be removed later):

> 1 stick cinnamon
>
> 4 whole cloves
>
> 4 peppercorns

Place the bundled spices in a heavy 3-quart soup pot along with:

> 5 cups water
>
> 1½ cups dry green split peas
>
> 1½ cups chopped onions
>
> 1 cup chopped tomato
>
> 1 chili pepper, seeded and minced
>
> 2 teaspoons ground coriander
>
> 2 teaspoons ground cumin
>
> 1 teaspoon turmeric
>
> ½ teaspoon ground ginger
>
> ½ teaspoon garlic powder
>
> ½ teaspoon ground cardamom
>
> ½ teaspoon chili powder

Bring to a boil, reduce the heat, and simmer, partially covered, for 1½ hours. The split peas should become soft and begin to disintegrate. Remove the bundled spices before serving. After the soup has finished cooking, add:

> salt to taste

yields 4 servings

per serving:

calories 196

protein 13 g

fat 0 g

carb 36 g

fiber 13 g

sodium 5 mg

yellow split pea
soup

Combine in a heavy 4-quart soup pot:

> 8 cups water
> 2 cups (1 pound) dry yellow split peas

I like to have a batch of muffins or chewy bread on hand to eat with this soup, as it lends itself to dunking. The subtle mint flavor makes this soup truly special.

Bring to a boil, reduce the heat, partially cover, and cook until soft, about 1 hour.

In a medium skillet, sauté for 3 to 5 minutes:

> 1½ cups chopped onions
> 1 tablespoon minced garlic
> 1 chili pepper, seeded and minced (optional)

> 1 teaspoon paprika
> 1 teaspoon ground coriander
> 1 teaspoon olive oil

Stir in:

> 2 cups chopped fresh or canned tomatoes
> 2 tablespoons tomato paste

Simmer for 20 minutes.

When the yellow split peas are soft enough to start falling apart, add the tomato and onion mixture along with:

> 2 tablespoons fresh lemon juice
> 1 tablespoon chopped fresh mint, or 1 teaspoon dried mint
> salt to taste

Bring to a boil, reduce the heat, and simmer, stirring occasionally, for 15 minutes.

yields 6 servings

per serving:

calories 199
protein 12 g
fat 2 g
carb 35 g
fiber 13 g
sodium 24 mg

kidney, garbanzo,
and white bean noodle soup

Fill a medium saucepan partway with water and bring to a boil. When boiling, add:

   ¾ cup noodles, small shells, or elbow macaroni

Cook 6 minutes, then drain and set aside.

Heat in a 3- to 4-quart soup pot:

   1 teaspoon olive oil

When hot, add and sauté until soft:

   1 cup chopped onions
   2 cloves garlic, minced
   1½ chili peppers, seeded and minced, or ¼ teaspoon
      dried red pepper flakes

Stir in:

   2 cups water or bean broth
   1½ cups tomato purée
   1 cup cooked white beans
   1 cup cooked red kidney beans
   1 cup cooked garbanzos beans
   1 teaspoon dried mint
   1 teaspoon dried dill weed
   ½ teaspoon salt

Bring to a boil, then reduce the heat, add the reserved noodles, and simmer for 5 minutes. Serve immediately or the noodles will become overcooked.

You can use a variety of leftover beans to create interesting textures and flavors in this thick and hearty soup.

yields 5 servings

per serving:
calories 256
protein 13 g
fat 3 g
carb 47 g
fiber 9 g
sodium 125 mg

black bean
soup

Eating black beans, dark and warming, is comforting any time of the year. With or without the scoop of rice, cornmeal muffins go well with this soup.

Soak overnight:

> 8 cups water
>
> 2 cups (1 pound) dry black beans

Drain and rinse. Combine the soaked beans in a 4-quart soup pot with:

> 8 cups fresh water
>
> 1 large onion, finely chopped
>
> 1 green bell pepper, chopped
>
> 1 bay leaf

Simmer for 1½ to 2 hours until the beans are very soft.

Add:

> 2 tablespoons fresh lemon juice
>
> 2 teaspoons ground cumin
>
> 1 teaspoon dried oregano
>
> salt to taste

Cook for 5 more minutes. Serve with a scoop of cooked rice in the middle of each bowl, if you wish, and garnish with chopped scallions.

yields 6 servings

per serving:

calories 204
protein 11 g
fat 1 g
carb 38 g
fiber 13 g
sodium 3 mg

creamy pinto
soup

Heat in a 3-quart soup pot:

> ½ teaspoon olive oil

When hot, add and sauté until tender:

> ⅔ cup chopped onions
> 1 chili or jalapeño pepper, seeded and minced
> 1 clove garlic, minced

Stir in:

> 3 cups cooked pinto beans
> 2 cups bean broth or water
> 1½ cups chopped fresh or canned tomatoes
> ½ teaspoon ground cumin
> ½ teaspoon dried oregano
> salt to taste

Bring to a boil, reduce the heat, and simmer for 10 minutes. Purée the soup in a food processor, blending a few cups of the soup at a time. Return to the pot, cover, and warm over low heat until ready to serve. Garnish with crumbled corn chips, if desired.

yields 4 servings

per serving:

calories 204
protein 11 g
fat 1 g
carb 38 g
fiber 123 g
sodium 9 mg

pasta plus pintos
soup

You are certain to like this combination of greens, pintos, and noodles. It's a wholesome meal in one dish, and you can choose which greens and pasta to use.

Heat in a 4-quart soup pot:

> 1 teaspoon olive oil

When hot, add and sauté until tender:

> 1 cup chopped onions
> 1 cup chopped celery
> 3 cloves garlic, minced

Stir in:

> 4 to 5 cups (1 pound) chopped spinach, kale, or collards
> 3 cups cooked pinto beans
> 3 cups water
> 3 cups low-sodium tomato juice

Bring to a boil. Stir in:

> 1 cup uncooked pasta, macaroni, or small shells
> salt to taste

Return to a boil, then reduce the heat to medium and simmer for 10 minutes, stirring occasionally. Remove from the heat, cover, and let rest for 5 minutes before serving.

yields 6 servings

per serving:

calories 225
protein 12 g
fat 2 g
carb 42 g
fiber 11 g
sodium 97 mg

more fabulous beans

sprouted lentil
soup

The sprouted lentils in this soup add a crisp texture that contrasts nicely with the cooked vegetables. Using miso in this recipe imparts a rich flavor that enhances the leeks and dill.

Heat in a 4-quart soup pot:

½ teaspoon olive oil

When hot, add and sauté until brown:

2 cloves garlic, minced

Stir in:

4 cups vegetable broth, bean broth, or water
1 cup chopped leeks
1 cup chopped carrots
1 cup chopped potatoes

Simmer for 15 minutes. Then stir in:

3 cups sprouted lentils (see page 50)
2 tablespoons chopped fresh dill weed,
   or 1 teaspoon dried dill weed

Bring to a boil. Remove from the heat and stir in:

3 tablespoons dark (mugi) miso

Mix until the miso has dissolved. Cover and let rest for 5 minutes before serving.

yields 5 servings

per serving:

calories 125
protein 6 g
fat 1 g
carb 25 g
fiber 3 g
sodium 396 mg

hearty split pea, lentil,
soybean 'n grain soup

This filling soup is one you'll want to prepare on cold winter evenings to keep you warm. The chewy barley and fragrant rosemary give it a distinctive flavor.

Combine in a 4-quart soup pot:

  6 cups water

  ½ cup pearl barley

  ½ cup bulgur

  ½ cup dry split peas

  ½ cup dry lentils

  1 onion, chopped

  2 cloves garlic, chopped

  1 bay leaf

Bring to a boil, reduce the heat, partially cover, and simmer for 50 minutes. Stir in:

  2 cups chopped fresh spinach

  1 cup cooked soybeans or other cooked beans

  2 tablespoons tamari

  ¼ teaspoon dried rosemary

Continue cooking 20 minutes longer. Add more water if the soup becomes too thick.

yields 6 servings

per serving:

calories 251

protein 18 g

fat 6 g

carb 36 g

fiber 12 g

sodium 355 mg

russian beet
and white kidney soup

Look for beets with fresh-looking greens attached so you can add them to this soup. If you like beets, you're sure to want to make this often.

Combine in a medium saucepan:

  4 cups water
  2½ cups thinly sliced small potatoes
  2 cups thinly sliced fresh beets

Bring to a boil, reduce the heat, cover and simmer for 8 to 10 minutes.

In a 4-quart soup pot, sauté until brown:

  1 large onion, chopped   1 teaspoon olive oil

Stir in·

  3 cups water   1 large carrot, cut into ¼-inch
  3 cups chopped cabbage   rounds
  2 stalks celery, chopped

Bring to a slow boil and cook, covered, for 10 minutes. Then stir in:

  2 cups cooked white kidney beans
  2 cups chopped beet greens
  2 tablespoons turbinado sugar or pure maple syrup
  2 tablespoons apple cider vinegar
  2 tablespoons fresh dill weed or 2 teaspoons dried dill weed
  1½ teaspoons whole caraway seeds
  Salt and pepper to taste

Cover and cook for 10 more minutes. Remove from the heat and keep covered until ready to serve.

yields 6 servings

per serving:

calories 212
protein 9 g
fat 1 g
carb 44 g
fiber 8 g
sodium 100 mg

black-eye butternut
chowder

Enjoy this warming winter soup with some dark bread and a leafy green salad.

Heat in a 3- to 4-quart soup pot:

> 1 teaspoon olive oil

When hot, add and sauté until beginning to brown:

> 1 cup chopped onions
> 1 cup chopped green peppers

Then add:

> 2 cups water
> 2 cups cubed potatoes

Cook until the potatoes are tender. Stir in:

> 1 cup frozen peas
> 1 cup frozen corn
> 1 tablespoon chili powder
> 2 teaspoons ground cumin

Cook for 3 minutes. Stir in:

> 4 cups puréed butternut squash
> 1½ cups cooked black-eyed peas
> salt to taste

Bring to a simmer. Stir in:

> 3 tablespoons fresh lime juice

Remove from the heat and serve.

yields 4 to 6 servings

per serving:

calories 256
protein 10 g
fat 2 g
carb 56 g
fiber 12 g
sodium 16 mg

white bean
chowder

There is no need to open a can to enjoy the treat of chowder.

Soak overnight:

> 4 cups water
> 1 cup dry navy beans

Drain and transfer to a 4-quart soup pot. Add:

> 3 cups fresh water.

Bring to boil, reduce the heat, cover, and simmer for 30 minutes. Add:

> 1 cup puréed tomatoes
> 2 medium potatoes, cubed (peeling is optional)
> 2 carrots, diced
> ¾ cup chopped onions
> 2 stalks celery, diced

Cook 35 minutes longer. Remove 3 cups of the bean and vegetable mixture, purée it in a food processor or blender, and return it to the simmering soup.

Stirring constantly, add:

> 2 cups soymilk
> 2 tablespoons chopped fresh parsley
> 1 tablespoon nutritional yeast flakes
> ⅛ teaspoon pepper
> 1 teaspoon salt (optional)

Let the soup simmer for a few minutes until it thickens.

yields 6 servings

per serving:

calories 192
protein 10 g
fat 2 g
carb 35 g
fiber 7 g
sodium 100 mg

lentil soup
with greens

This soup is like a hearty stew. Enjoy it with a chunk of corn bread or crusty Italian bread.

Rinse well:

> 1½ cups dry lentils

Transfer to a 4-quart soup pot and add:

> 8 cups water

Bring to a boil, then lower the heat and simmer gently for 45 minutes.

Heat in a medium skillet:

> 1 teaspoon canola oil

When hot, add and sauté for 5 minutes:

> 1 cup chopped onions
> 3 cloves garlic, minced

Add to the cooked lentils, along with:

> 6 cups (1½ pounds) chopped greens (spinach, Swiss chard, collards, or kale)
> ¼ cup chopped fresh parsley
> 2 tablespoons tomato paste
> ½ teaspoon ground cumin
> ½ teaspoon dried red pepper flakes
> salt to taste

Stir well. Cook over medium heat for 15 minutes.

yields 6 servings

per serving:

calories 165
protein 13 g
fat 5 g
carb 28 g
fiber 12 g
sodium 109 mg

pinto, navy, and lima
bean soup

The fresh parsley and basil give these mixed beans a special flavor. Topped with roasted sunflower seeds, this soup is spectacular.

Soak overnight:

> 5 cups water
> ½ cup dry pinto beans
> ½ cup dry navy beans
> ½ cup dry lima beans

Drain and rinse. Transfer to a 4-quart soup pot and add:

> 5 cups fresh water

Bring to a boil, reduce the heat, cover and cook for 1 hour.

In a medium skillet, sauté until soft:

> 1 cup chopped onions
> 1 cup chopped celery
> 1 green bell pepper, chopped
> 1 chili pepper, seeded and chopped
> 1 teaspoon olive oil

Add to the beans, along with:

> ⅓ cup chopped fresh parsley
> 1 tablespoon chopped fresh basil, or 1 teaspoon dried basil
> ½ teaspoon ground coriander

Cover and simmer about 1 hour or until everything is tender. Season with:

> salt to taste

Before serving, garnish with:

> ½ cup coarsely ground, roasted sunflower seeds (optional)

yields 4 to 6 servings

per serving:

calories 173
protein 10 g
fat 2 g
carb 32 g
fiber 9 g
sodium 26 mg

white bean summer
minestrone

When garden produce is available, this soup offers a special freshness. How can you resist the deluge of vegetables that are transformed into this scrumptious soup?

In a 4-quart soup pot, sauté until lightly browned:

>   1 cup finely chopped onions
>   1 tablespoon minced garlic
>   1 teaspoon olive oil

Stir in:

>   5 cups vegetable stock, bean stock, or water
>   4 cups chopped tomatoes
>   1 cup soaked and drained white beans, or 2½ cups cooked white beans*
>   1 cup sliced green beans (1-inch pieces)
>   1 cup diced zucchini
>   1 cup diced potatoes

>   ¾ cup sliced carrots
>   ½ cup chopped celery
>   ⅓ cup long grain rice
>   ¼ cup chopped fresh parsley
>   2 tablespoons chopped fresh basil, or 2 teaspoons dried basil
>   ¾ teaspoon dried sage
>   ¾ teaspoon dried rosemary
>   1 bay leaf

Bring to a gentle boil, cover, and cook for 1 hour, stirring occasionally. Add:

>   salt to taste

*If using cooked beans, add them to the soup with the salt. Simmer until the beans are heated through.

yields 6 to 8 servings

per serving:

calories 182
protein 9 g
fat 1 g
carb 36 g
fiber 8 g
sodium 27 mg

more fabulous beans

creamy corn and lima
soup

My kids love this creamy soup that is rich with corn and seasoned with a dash of dill.

Combine in a food processor or blender:

> 3 cups cooked lima beans
> 3 cups bean broth or water

Set aside. Heat in a 3- to 4-quart soup pot:

> 1 teaspoon canola oil

When hot, add and sauté until soft:

> ¾ cup chopped onions

Add:

> 2 cups fresh or frozen corn

Cook until hot. Stir in:

> 2 tablespoons unbleached white flour
> 2 tablespoons chopped fresh dill weed, or 1 teaspoon dried dill weed
> ½ teaspoon salt (optional)
> ⅛ teaspoon pepper

Gradually stir in:

> 1½ cups soymilk

Stir or whisk to dissolve any lumps, and simmer for 3 minutes. Then add the bean purée, and heat gently until hot throughout. Serve immediately.

yields 5 servings

per serving:

calories 242
protein 13 g
fat 3 g
carb 44 g
fiber 11 g
sodium 16 mg

split pea
soup

This soup is one of our favorites. The chilled leftovers make a tasty spread on bread or crackers.

Rinse:

>   2 cups (1 pound) dry split peas

Place in a 4-quart soup pot and add:

>   2 quarts cold water
>   2 cups peeled and cubed sweet potatoes
>   1 cup chopped onions
>   1 cup chopped celery
>   2 cloves garlic, minced
>   1 bay leaf
>   ¼ teaspoon dried thyme

Bring to a boil, reduce the heat, partially cover, and simmer, stirring occasionally, until the split peas are soft, about 1 to 1½ hours. Season with:

>   salt and pepper to taste

If you prefer a smooth, creamy soup, purée it in a food processor.

yields 6 servings

per serving:

calories 221
protein 12 g
fat 1 g
carb 43 g
fiber 13 g
sodium 19 mg

lima and split pea
composite soup

This lovely composite of beans, grains, and vegetables lets you create a meal in one pot. If you have other vegetables on hand that you'd like to substitute, try them.

Combine in a 4-quart soup pot:

> 7 cups water
> 1 cup dry baby lima beans
> ½ cup dry yellow split peas

Bring to a boil, reduce the heat, partially cover, and cook for 35 minutes.
Add:

> ¼ cup pearl barley
> ¼ cup brown rice

Cover and continue to cook for 25 minutes. Then add:

> 2 cups tomato purée or juice
> 1 cup chopped carrots
> 1 cup chopped celery
> 1 cup chopped mushrooms
> 1 onion, chopped
> 1 potato, cubed (peeling is optional)

Simmer for 20 minutes. Stir in:

> ¼ cup chopped fresh dill weed, or 4 teaspoons dried dill
> ¼ cup chopped fresh parsley
> 1 teaspoon salt (optional)
> ¼ teaspoon pepper

Cook on low heat for 5 minutes. Remove from the heat, cover, and let rest for a few minutes before serving. Serve hot.

yields 6 to 8 servings

per serving:
calories 192
protein 10 g
fat 1 g
carb 38 g
fiber 10 g
sodium 131 mg

white bean karhi
and chickpea flour pakoris

Sift into a bowl:

⅜ cup (6 tablespoons) chickpea flour*

Combine in a blender:

¾ cup cooked white beans
½ cup water
2 teaspoons apple cider vinegar

Purée until smooth. Gradually stir into the chickpea flour, mixing well to form a thick, smooth paste. Add to the paste:

2½ cups water

Mix well, and set aside.

Heat in a heavy-bottomed 3-quart soup pot:

1 teaspoon canola oil

When hot, add:

⅛ teaspoon whole fennel seeds
⅛ teaspoon black mustard seeds
⅛ teaspoon whole cumin seeds
pinch of whole fenugreek seeds

Chickpea flour can be found in Indian groceries, where it is called besan. It is also available in natural food stores.

This Indian dish, traditionally made with buttermilk, is a thick soup with dumplings that is usually eaten with plain rice. The sour and spicy flavor of this dish is a real treat.

Stir while the seeds start to pop. When the seeds are fragrant and a shade darker, add:

    ½ teaspoon turmeric flakes
    ¼ teaspoon dried red pepper

Add the bean and chickpea flour mixture. Bring to a boil, lower the heat, cover, and simmer gently for 1 hour, stirring occasionally.

Season with:

    1 to 1½ tablespoons fresh lemon juice
    ½ teaspoon salt (optional)

Cover and cook 10 minutes longer.

While the karhi is cooking, make the pakoris (next page).

When the karhi is done, carefully put the dumplings in the soup. Just before serving, gently warm the karhi and pakoris. Serve hot over rice.

yields 3 to 4
servings

per serving
(with pakoris):

calories 149
protein 9 g
fat 3 g
carb 25 g
fiber 5 g
sodium 29 mg

pakoris
(dumplings)

These can be made while the karhi is cooking (yields 6 to 8 dumplings).

Sift into a bowl:

> ½ cup chickpea flour
> ¼ teaspoon baking powder
> ¼ teaspoon ground cumin
> ¼ teaspoon salt (optional)

Add slowly, stirring constantly:

> ¼ cup water

Mix thoroughly to create a thick, doughy paste. Heat a skillet or wok over medium heat. Put a few drops of oil in the skillet, and spread it with a spatula to cover the bottom. Drop the batter in lumps using a teaspoon; use a second spoon to release the paste.

Lower the heat and cook the dumplings slowly, turning a few times to cook them evenly. The dumplings should maintain their yellowish color. Don't cook them until they turn brown.

Have a bowl of warm water ready. When the dumplings are done, lift them into the warm water, and let them soak for 2 minutes. Remove the dumplings from the water, and squeeze them very gently, taking care not to break them. Cover and set aside.

chilis and stews

kidney bean
chili pepper chili

Dried peppers impart a rich red hue to the sauce of this chili. You can decide how many peppers to use. How hot can you take it? We like to eat chili with corn bread and tossed salad.

Remove the seeds and tear into large pieces:

  3 to 6 dried red chili peppers

Place them in a bowl and add:

  ½ cup boiling water

Cover the bowl and let them soak for 10 to 15 minutes.

Transfer the soaked peppers and the soaking water to a blender and process into a smooth paste. Set aside.

In a large skillet, cook over medium heat for several minutes, stirring occasionally:

  1 onion, finely chopped
  1 bell pepper, finely chopped
  1 cup finely chopped celery
  1 teaspoon olive oil

Add to the skillet along with the reserved chili paste:

  3 cups tomato purée or chopped tomatoes
  3 cups cooked kidney beans
  1½ cups fresh or frozen corn
  2 teaspoons ground cumin
  1 teaspoon garlic powder
  Salt to taste

Stir and bring to a boil. Reduce the heat and simmer, stirring occasionally, for 5 to 10 minutes or until the chili thickens. Serve hot.

yields 4 to 6 servings

per serving:

calories 215
protein 12 g
fat 2 g
carb 42 g
fiber 11 g
sodium 213 mg

more fabulous beans

black bean eggplant *chili*

Even with a few surprise ingredients, this chili is a snap to make. The eggplant and bulgur add a chewy texture.

In a large, heavy skillet sauté for 5 minutes::

> 1 medium eggplant, cut into bite-sized pieces (about 4 cups)
> 1 medium onion, chopped
> 1 bell pepper, chopped
> 1 teaspoon olive oil

Stir in:

> 4 cups cooked black beans
> 29 ounces tomato purée or chopped tomatoes
> 1 cup water
> ½ cup bulgur
> 1 tablespoon ground cumin
> 1 tablespoon chili powder
> 1 teaspoon dried oregano
> 1 teaspoon garlic powder
> salt to taste

Bring to a boil, reduce the heat, and simmer, stirring occasionally, for 10 minutes. Remove from the heat and cover until ready to serve.

yields 6 to 8 servings

per serving:

calories 231
protein 13 g
fat 2 g
carb 44 g
fiber 15 g
sodium 208 mg

white bean and squash
stew

Serve this appetizing stew over rice or bulgur.

Combine in a 3- to 4-quart soup pot: (omit this step if using cooked beans)

　　4 cups water
　　1½ cups dry white beans

Bring to a boil, reduce the heat, cover, and simmer for 30 minutes.

Stir in:

　　2 medium potatoes, chopped (peeling is optional)
　　2 cups peeled and cubed winter squash or pumpkin
　　1 large onion, chopped
　　1 cup chopped fresh or canned tomatoes
　　2 leeks, chopped
　　2 cloves garlic, chopped
　　*1 cup water (if using cooked beans to be added later)

Cover and cook, stirring occasionally, for 30 to 45 minutes or until the beans and vegetables are soft. Add:

　　*3 cups cooked beans (if not using dry beans)
　　6 to 8 tablespoons fresh lemon juice
　　¼ cup chopped fresh parsley
　　3 tablespoons tomato paste
　　salt to taste
　　½ teaspoon whole dill seed

Cover and simmer for 10 minutes longer. Remove from the heat and keep covered until ready to serve.

yields 4 to 6 servings

per serving:

calories 298
protein 14 g
fat 1 g
carb 62 g
fiber 13 g
sodium 55 mg

butter bean
irish stew

You'll taste the sweetness of parsnips in this chewy barley dish.

In a heavy-bottomed 3-quart pot, sauté for 5 minutes or until lightly browned:

2 parsnips, cut into bite-size pieces
2 medium carrots, cut into bite-size pieces
1 medium turnip, cut into bite-size pieces
1 onion, cut into bite-size pieces
1 teaspoon olive oil

Add:

3 cups water
1 cup pearl barley

Simmer for 15 minutes. Stir in:

2 cups cut green beans (in bite-size pieces)
¾ teaspoon dried thyme

Cover and simmer for 5 minutes. Stir in:

1½ cups cooked butter beans or lima beans
1 cup frozen green peas
Salt and pepper to taste

Add more water to prevent sticking, if necessary. Cover and heat through before serving.

yields 4 servings

per serving:

calories 340
protein 12 g
fat 2 g
carb 72 g
fiber 18 g
sodium 51 mg

autumn lima bean
and split pea stew

In a 3-quart soup pot, sauté until soft:

> ¾ cup chopped onions
> 1 large clove garlic, chopped
> 1 teaspoon olive oil

Stir in:

> 5 cups water
> 2 cups peeled and cubed sweet potatoes
> 2 cups chopped green cabbage
> ½ cup dry lima beans
> ½ cup bulgur
> ¼ cup dry yellow split peas
> 1 tablespoon tamari
> ¼ teaspoon dried rosemary

Bring to a boil, lower the heat, cover, and simmer, stirring occasionally, for about 1 hour or until the beans are soft.

yields 4 to 6 servings

per serving:

calories 173
protein 8 g
fat 1 g
carb 34 g
fiber 9 g
sodium 215 mg

garbanzo
spanish stew

In a 4-quart soup pot, sauté until soft:

> 2 cups sliced mushrooms
> 1 cup thinly sliced cabbage
> 1 onion, thinly sliced
> 4 cloves garlic, minced
> 1 teaspoon olive oil

Add:

> 3 cups puréed tomatoes
> 2 carrots, thinly sliced
> 1 potato, diced (peeling is optional)
> 1 bay leaf

Bring to a boil, reduce the heat, cover, and simmer for 15 minutes. Stir in:

> 2 cups cooked or canned garbanzo beans
> 2 tablespoons minced fresh parsley
> 1 tablespoon chopped fresh mint
> 1 teaspoon dried oregano
> 1 teaspoon salt (optional)
> ⅛ teaspoon pepper

Simmer for 10 minutes.

yields 6 servings

per serving:

calories 196
protein 9 g
fat 3 g
carb 37 g
fiber 8 g
sodium 215 mg

lentil-vegetable
biryani

Sauté in a heavy 3- to 4-quart soup pot until golden:

  1 cup chopped onions
  ½ teaspoon canola oil

Stir in:

  8 cloves garlic, minced
  2 chili peppers, seeded and minced
  1½-inch piece fresh gingerroot, grated

Sauté for 3 minutes. Add:

  3 large potatoes, cut into ½-inch cubes (peeling is optional)
  2 large tomatoes, chopped into 1-inch pieces, or 2 cups
      canned chopped tomatoes
  1½ cups water
  1 cup green beans, cut into bite-sized pieces
  1 cup sliced carrots
  ¾ cup soaked lentils, drained
  1 stick cinnamon
  1 teaspoon turmeric
  ½ teaspoon ground cardamom
  4 whole cloves

This potpourri of vegetables, spices, and lentils produces a memorable dish. Serve this when you have company or whenever you want something especially nutritious and delicious.

Bring to a boil, lower the heat, cover, and cook for 15 minutes. Add:

  3 cups hot water
  1 cup white basmati rice
  1 cup fresh or frozen green peas
  2 tablespoons minced fresh mint, or ½ teaspoon dried mint
  ½ teaspoon salt (optional)

Cover and cook 25 to 30 minutes or until the rice is tender. Remove from the heat and let rest, covered, for 5 to 10 minutes before serving.

yields 4 to 6 servings

per serving:

calories 297
protein 12 g
fat 1 g
carb 61 g
fiber 11 g
sodium 22 mg

kidney-polenta
stew

Leftover polenta is delicious the next day. It gets firm when cold, so you can slice and lightly fry it. Try topping it with a little tomato sauce, if desired.

Combine in a heavy-bottomed 3-quart soup pot:

    1 quart of water
    ¾ cup cornmeal
    ¾ cup chopped onions
    ¾ cup chopped celery
    1 tablespoon tamari
    2 cloves garlic, chopped
    1 bay leaf

Bring to a boil, reduce the heat, and simmer for 20 minutes, stirring occasionally. Then add:

    2 cups cooked kidney beans
    1 (10-ounce) package frozen spinach, thawed
    ½ teaspoon salt (optional)

Simmer until heated through. Serve immediately.

yields 6 servings

per serving:

calories 155
protein 9 g
fat 1 g
carb 30 g
fiber 7 g
sodium 228 mg

more fabulous beans

lentil
stew

Sauté in a 3-quart soup pot until soft:

1 cup chopped onions	½ cup diced carrots
½ cup chopped celery	1 teaspoon olive oil

Stir in:

4 cups water	½ teaspoon dried oregano
1 cup dry lentils	½ teaspoon dried thyme
1 teaspoon dried basil	

Bring to a boil, reduce the heat, cover, and simmer for 45 minutes.

Meanwhile, cook in a medium skillet:

1 medium eggplant, cubed
1 teaspoon olive oil

Turn frequently to lightly brown on all sides.

When the lentils are soft, add:

1 (6-ounce) can tomato paste	¼ teaspoon ground cinnamon
¼ cup balsamic vinegar	pinch of dried red pepper flakes
½ teaspoon salt	

Stir in the browned eggplant, cover, and cook on low heat for 10 minutes. Add a little water if the stew is too thick.

yields 6 servings

per serving:

calories 144
protein 8 g
fat 2 g
carb 25 g
fiber 9 g
sodium 92 mg

kidney-yam
stew

Combine in a 4-quart soup pot:

> 5 cups water
>
> 2 cups peeled and cubed yams or sweet potatoes
>
> 2 medium white potatoes, cubed (peeling is optional)
>
> 1 cup chopped green beans (if using canned green beans, add them later with corn and kidney beans)
>
> 1 cup chopped cabbage
>
> 1 cup chopped fresh or canned tomatoes
>
> ½ cup brown rice
>
> 1 medium onion, chopped
>
> 1 green bell pepper, chopped
>
> 1 jalapeño pepper, seeded and minced (optional)
>
> 2 cloves garlic, minced

Bring to a boil, reduce the heat, cover, and simmer for 30 minutes. Stir in:

> 2 cups cooked kidney beans
>
> 1 cup fresh or frozen corn
>
> ¼ cup chopped fresh parsley or cilantro or a combination of both
>
> 1 teaspoon salt (optional)

Simmer 15 minutes longer, stirring occasionally. Add some bean stock or water if the stew is too thick.

yields 6 servings

per serving:

calories 255

protein 10 g

fat 1 g

carb 55 g

fiber 10 g

sodium 19 mg

more fabulous beans

garbanzo-sweet potato
stew

This stew is delicious served over couscous or brown rice.

In a heavy 3- to 4-quart soup pot, sauté until soft:

    1 cup chopped onions
    1 cup chopped red or green bell pepper
    1½ chili peppers, seeded and minced
    1 teaspoon olive oil

Stir in:

    2 cups chopped tomatoes
    2 cups peeled and cubed sweet potato
    ¼ cup water
    ½ teaspoon ground cinnamon
    ½ teaspoon ground coriander
    ½ teaspoon ground cardamom

Cover and simmer for 10 minutes. Add:

    2 cups cooked or canned garbanzo beans
    2 cups chopped zucchini
    3 to 4 tablespoons fresh lemon juice
    ½ teaspoon salt (optional)

Cover and cook 10 minutes longer.

yields 6 servings

per serving:

calories 183
protein 7 g
fat 3 g
carb 35 g
fiber 7 g
sodium 15 mg

easy white bean *stew*

This recipe is a great way to use up leftover beans.

In a 3- to 4-quart soup pot, bring to a boil:

> 2 cups bean or vegetable stock or water

Add:

> 2 potatoes, cubed (peeling is optional)
> 1 cup chopped carrots
> 1 bay leaf

Reduce the heat and simmer for 5 to 10 minutes.

Sauté in a medium skillet until the cabbage is soft:

> 2 cups sliced cabbage
> 1 cup chopped onions
> 1 cup halved mushrooms
> 1 cup chopped green or red bell peppers
> 3 cloves garlic, minced
> 1 teaspoon canola oil

Stir in:

> 2 cups cooked white beans
> 1 tablespoon fresh lemon juice
> 1 tablespoon dried chervil
> 1 teaspoon dried thyme
> ½ teaspoon salt (optional)
> pepper to taste

Simmer for 5 minutes. Remove from the heat, cover, and let rest for 15 minutes before serving.

yields 6 servings

per serving:

calories 165
protein 8 g
fat 1 g
carb 32 g
fiber 7 g
sodium 20 mg

lentils
'n barley

The hearty texture of this super quick and easy dish makes it stand out.

Combine in a 3-quart soup pot:

    1½ cups low-sodium tomato juice
    1 cup water
    ½ cup dry lentils
    ⅓ cup pearl barley

Bring to a boil, reduce the heat, cover, and simmer for 15 minutes. Stir in:

    1 cup chopped celery
    ½ cup chopped onions
    ½ cup chopped carrots
    ½ cup peeled and diced potatoes
    ½ teaspoon dried savory
    ½ teaspoon dried chervil
    ½ teaspoon dried thyme
    ½ teaspoon dried tarragon

Cover and simmer for 25 minutes, stirring occasionally. If the stew sticks to the bottom of the pot, add a little more water.

yields 4 servings

per serving:

calories 142
protein 6 g
fat 0 g
carb 29 g
fiber 7 g
sodium 101 mg

garbanzo *gumbo*

You can use fresh or frozen okra for this colorful dish, which is traditionally served over rice. Our southern cousins will be proud of this alternative to their familiar stew.

In a 4-quart soup pot, sauté for 5 minutes:

>   4 cups sliced okra (cut in ½-inch rounds)
>   1 cup chopped onions
>   1 green pepper, chopped
>   1 green chili pepper, seeded and finely chopped
>   3 cloves garlic, minced
>   1 teaspoon olive oil

Stir in:

>   3 cups chopped fresh or canned tomatoes
>   ½ cup chopped fresh parsley
>   ¼ cup chopped fresh basil, or ½ teaspoon dried basil

Simmer until the okra is tender. Then add:

>   3 cups cooked garbanzo beans
>   1 to 1½ cups bean stock, as needed

Add just enough stock to make a gravy. Bring to a boil, reduce the heat, and season with:

>   3 tablespoons fresh lemon juice
>   ½ teaspoon salt (optional)

Simmer for a few minutes, and keep hot until ready to serve.

yields 6 servings

per serving:

calories 205
protein 10 g
fat 3 g
carb 36 g
fiber 9 g
sodium 23 mg

burgers, balls, and wraps

soy *burgers*

These are a favorite with my family. The patties can be made in advance and refrigerated until you're ready to cook them. Serve them on buns with lettuce or sprouts and tomato.

Mash with a potato masher or in a food processor.

> 4 cups cooked soybeans

Stir in:

> ½ cup chopped onions, or 1 teaspoon onion powder
> ¼ cup chopped fresh parsley, or 1 tablespoon dried parsley
> ⅓ cup wheat germ
> 1 tablespoon tamari
> 1 teaspoon garlic powder
> ½ teaspoon dried oregano

Mix well until thoroughly combined. Wet your hands to keep the mixture from sticking to them and form into patties. Cook on a hot, lightly oiled skillet until brown on both sides.

yields 12 burgers

per burger:

calories 115
protein 11 g
fat 5 g
carb 8 g
fiber 4 g
sodium 86 mg

lentil *burgers*

Combine in a medium saucepan:

> 3 cups water
> 1 cup dry lentils

Bring to a boil, reduce the heat, cover, and cook for 30 minutes or until tender. Drain and transfer to a large bowl.

Steam-fry in a medium skillet, stirring often to prevent sticking:

> 1 small onion, finely chopped
> 4 mushrooms (⅓ cup), chopped
> 1 stalk celery, minced
> 1 tablespoon water

When tender, add to the cooked lentils along with:

> ¼ cup unbleached flour
> ¼ cup rolled oats or grated fresh bread crumbs
> 2 tablespoons peanut butter or tahini
> 1 teaspoon dried oregano
> 1 teaspoon prepared mustard
> ½ teaspoon dried thyme
> ½ teaspoon dried sage
> ½ teaspoon garlic powder
> ¼ teaspoon salt (optional)

Mix thoroughly until well combined. Shape into 8 patties and fry in an oiled skillet until brown on both sides. Alternatively, bake on an oiled cookie sheet in a 350°F oven for 20 minutes, turning once to brown both sides.

yields 8 burgers

per burger:

calories 111
protein 7 g
fat 2 g
carb 17 g
fiber 5 g
sodium 23 mg

pinto *burgers*

Combine in a small bowl:

> ⅔ cup dry textured vegetable protein granules
>
> ½ cup boiling water

Let rest for 10 minutes. Then stir in:

> 2 teaspoons tamari
>
> 1 teaspoon garlic powder
>
> ½ teaspoon dried oregano
>
> ½ teaspoon chili powder
>
> ⅛ teaspoon pepper

In a small skillet, sauté until soft:

> ⅔ cup minced onions
>
> ½ teaspoon olive oil

Transfer to a medium bowl and add:

> 2 cups cooked pinto beans, mashed
>
> ¾ cup cooked (cold) oatmeal

Add the textured vegetable protein and mix thoroughly until well combined. Wet hands with cold water and pat the mixture into thin burgers. Fry the burgers in an oiled skillet until brown on both sides.

These burgers are great for a quick supper when the kids are in and out. I like to keep leftover cooked oatmeal in the refrigerator to use as an egg substitute in cakes and cookies and for recipes like this one.

yields 12 burgers

per burger:

calories 68

protein 5 g

fat 1 g

carb 11 g

fiber 3 g

sodium 57 mg

curried pinto and veggie *fritters*

Combine in a medium mixing bowl:

- 1 cup cooked pinto beans, mashed
- 1 cup chopped celery
- ½ cup grated carrots
- ½ cup minced onions
- ½ cup water
- 1 tablespoon tamari

Stir to mix well. Sift into the bowl:

- ½ cup chickpea flour
- 1 teaspoon ground cumin
- 1 teaspoon baking powder
- ½ teaspoon garlic powder
- ¼ teaspoon ground coriander
- ¼ teaspoon ground cardamom

Mix until evenly combined. With damp hands, pat into flat, round patties, 3 inches in diameter. Cook in a lightly oiled, medium-hot skillet. Turn once to brown both sides. Alternatively, bake on an oiled cookie sheet in a 350°F oven for 10 minutes on each side.

These crunchy, curried fritters make handy travel food. They also are great for bag lunches or supper. I like them cooked in just a drop of oil, but you can make them crispier by using more oil. Have some chutney on hand to serve with them. Look for chickpea flour, also called besan, in Indian grocery stores.

*yields fourteen
3-inch fritters*

per 2 fritters:

calories 74
protein 4 g
fat 1 g
carb 14 g
fiber 4 g
sodium 163 mg

lima and navy bean
sausage links

These little links are delicious for breakfast, lunch, or dinner. Prepare the full recipe, store the mixture in the refrigerator, and cook the links as needed. You might want to freeze part of the mixture to have another time. We like to eat these with bagels.

Preheat the oven to 450°F. Oil a cookie sheet and set aside.

Combine and mash in a food processor:

> 2 cups cooked soybeans
>
> 1 cup cooked lima beans
>
> 1 cup cooked navy beans

Transfer to a large bowl and stir in:

> ½ cup wheat germ
>
> ½ cup whole wheat flour
>
> ½ cup nutritional yeast flakes
>
> 2 tablespoons tamari
>
> 2 tablespoons prepared mustard
>
> 1½ teaspoons whole fennel seeds
>
> 1½ tablespoons brown sugar
>
> 1 tablespoon dried oregano
>
> 4 teaspoons garlic powder
>
> 1 teaspoon ground allspice
>
> ½ teaspoon pepper
>
> ½ teaspoon cayenne
>
> ½ teaspoon salt (optional)

Mix well and shape into finger-size links or small patties. Arrange on the prepared baking sheet and bake for 10 to 15 minutes, turn over, and bake 10 to 15 minutes longer or until brown.

yields 36 links

per 2 links:

calories 100

protein 8 g

fat 2 g

carb 13 g

fiber 3 g

sodium 134 mg

more fabulous beans

kidney bean
sloppy joes

Here's an old favorite embellished by adding vegetables to the mix.

In a large skillet, sauté until soft but not mushy:

> 1 onion, chopped
>
> 2 carrots, chopped
>
> 1 zucchini, in small dice
>
> 1 green bell pepper, chopped
>
> 1 teaspoon olive oil

Stir in:

> 1½ cups cooked kidney beans
>
> 1 cup tomato purée
>
> ½ cup barbeque sauce
>
> 2 teaspoons chili powder
>
> 1 teaspoon paprika
>
> 1 teaspoon ground cumin
>
> 1 teaspoon garlic powder

Simmer for 15 minutes, stirring occasionally. Cover and remove from the heat. Serve over:

> 4 whole wheat buns, sliced

yields 4 servings

per serving (with bun):

calories 323
protein 14 g
fat 5 g
carb 62 g
fiber 10 g
sodium 437 mg

garbanzo *falafels*

Preheat the oven to 350°F.

Lightly oil a cookie sheet and set aside.

Combine in a food processor or mash in a bowl:

> 3 cups cooked garbanzo beans
> 1 small onion, finely chopped
> ¼ cup whole wheat flour
> ¼ cup minced fresh parsley
> 2 tablespoons wheat germ
> 1 teaspoon paprika
> 1 tablespoon tamari
> ¼ teaspoon garlic powder

Mix well. Wet hands and form into 1-inch balls. Place on the prepared cookie sheet as the balls are formed. Bake for 10 minutes, turn over, and bake 10 minutes longer.

High-protein falafels traditionally are served in pita bread with fresh vegetables, nondairy yogurt, and tahini sauce as toppings. These particular falafels are baked rather than fried, keeping them low in fat. If you have any leftovers, the balls can be flattened and used in sandwiches.

*yields twenty
1-inch balls*

per 2 balls:

calories 102
protein 5 g
fat 2 g
carb 18 g
fiber 4 g
sodium 105 mg

ratatouille roll-ups
with cannellini beans

The secret to this meal is to keep the vegetables crisp to impart a crunchy texture within the chewy wrap.

Heat in a medium skillet:

> 1 teaspoon olive oil

When hot, add:

> 1 medium eggplant, peeled and cubed
>
> 1 small zucchini, cut into bite-size pieces
>
> 1 onion, sliced into crescents
>
> 1 large green bell pepper, sliced into thin strips

Cover and cook, stirring occasionally, for 5 minutes. Stir in:

> 2 cups cooked cannellini beans
>
> ¾ cup pureed tomatoes
>
> 2 tablespoons balsamic vinegar
>
> 2 tablespoons tomato paste

> 2 teaspoons dried basil
>
> 1 teaspoon dried oregano
>
> ⅛ teaspoon pepper
>
> Salt to taste

Uncover and simmer, stirring occasionally, until thickened, about 5 minutes.

Warm:

> 6 whole wheat tortillas

Spread the hot vegetable mixture down the center of each tortilla. Sprinkle with:

> 1½ cups grated carrots

Roll up tightly and serve.

yields 6 roll-ups

per serving:

calories 218

protein 11 g

fat 2 g

carb 47 g

fiber 9 g

sodium 251 mg

butter bean veggie wraps
with peanut sauce

Have ready:

6 wraps

For the dressing, combine in a small jar with a tight fitting lid:

3 tablespoons chopped fresh cilantro
2 tablespoons fresh lime juice
1 tablespoon smooth peanut butter
1 tablespoon maple syrup
1 tablespoon tamari
1 tablespoon water
1 teaspoon grated fresh gingerroot

Shake vigorously until well combined. Set aside.

Sauté for 5 minutes in a medium skillet:

2 cups sliced mushrooms
1 yellow squash, sliced into ¼-inch rounds
1 red bell pepper, sliced into ⅓-inch strips
1 green bell pepper, sliced into ⅓-inch strips
1 onion, cut into crescents
1 teaspoon olive oil

Stir in:

1½ cups cooked butter beans
1 teaspoon chili powder
1 teaspoon dried basil

Remove from the heat and keep covered until ready to serve.

yields 6 wraps

*per serving
(filling only):*

calories 117
protein 6 g
fat 2 g
carb 20 g
fiber 5 g
sodium 179 mg

I usually use whole wheat tortillas for wraps, but rectangular wraps of different colors and flavors are fun to use, too. Use your imagination and substitute different vegetables for the filling. The peanut sauce brings this dish alive.

While the vegetables are cooking. heat the wraps individually on a skillet or arrange them in a single layer on a cookie sheet and heat them in the oven. Warm them only until they are soft, not crispy, or you will not be able to roll them. When you are ready to eat, remove the vegetables from the skillet using a slotted spoon and place a portion of them down the center of each wrap. Drizzle a small amount of the sauce over the vegetables and roll the wrap around them.

meatless pinto *balls*

Try these with spaghetti. They make good sandwich fillers if you have any left over.

Combine in a medium bowl:

2½ cups cooked pinto beans, mashed

¾ cup grated fresh bread crumbs

½ cup minced onions

¼ cup nutritional yeast flakes

¼ cup chopped fresh parsley

2 tablespoons tamari

1 teaspoon dried basil

1 teaspoon garlic powder

½ teaspoon whole celery seeds

¼ teaspoon ground allspice

yields 24 balls

per 2 balls:

calories 78

protein 6 g

fat 0 g

carb 14 g

fiber 4 g

sodium 185 mg

Mix with your hands until thoroughly combined. Roll into 1-inch balls and brown in a lightly oiled, covered skillet, turning a few times to brown all sides evenly.

dilled garbanzos in pitas
with baked vegetables

Baking vegetables in your oven frees you to attend to other kitchen activities. I love the crunchy results.

Preheat the oven to 400°F. Lightly oil 2 cookie sheets and set aside. Have ready:

> 6 pita breads, warmed and cut in half

Fill a medium saucepan partway with water and bring to a boil. Add:

> 3 cups diced peeled potatoes

Boil until almost soft. Drain well and spread in a single layer on the prepared cookie sheets along with:

> 2 zucchini, cut into bite-size pieces
> 1 red bell pepper, cut into bite-size pieces
> 1 green bell pepper, cut into bite-size pieces
> 1 onion, cut into bite-size pieces

In a small bowl, combine:

> 2 tablespoons spicy mustard
> 1 tablespoon olive oil
>
> 3 cloves garlic, minced
> 1 teaspoon dried basil

Mix well and sprinkle over the potatoes and vegetables. Bake for 15 minutes, stir or turn over the pieces, spread them out again in a single layer, and bake for 10 minutes longer.

Combine in a large bowl:

> 1½ cups cooked garbanzo beans
> ½ cup plain nondairy yogurt
>
> ¼ cup chopped fresh dill weed,
>   or 1 tablespoon dried dill weed
> 2 tablespoons soy mayonnaise

Stir in the baked vegetables and mix well. Stuff into pita breads and serve.

yields 6 stuffed pitas

per serving:
calories 318
protein 13 g
fat 6 g
carb 54 g
fiber 10 g
sodium 410 mg

just

beans

pat's baked
navy beans

Whip this together and make some potato salad while it's baking. This is a great dish to include in an outdoor menu. Be sure the kids are there; they'll love these baked beans.

Preheat the oven to 300°F.

Combine in a large bowl:

    3 cups cooked navy beans

    1 cup bean stock

    ⅓ cup light molasses

    ¼ cup brown sugar

    ¼ cup ketchup

    1 heaping tablespoon prepared yellow mustard

    1 small onion, diced, or 1 teaspoon onion powder

    ½ teaspoon garlic powder

Spoon into a shallow, 2-quart baking dish, and bake for about 45 minutes or until thickened but not dry.

yields 4 servings

per serving:

calories 340

protein 13 g

fat 1 g

carb 73 g

fiber 8 g

sodium 240 mg

soybeans
in sweet sauce

Have a hankering for something sweet but don't feel like making a dessert? Try this simple, yet unusual, combination. The molasses gives it a rich flavor.

Combine in a medium saucepan:

½ cup bean stock or water

3 tablespoons sweetener of your choice

1 tablespoon tamari

1 tablespoon cornstarch

1 tablespoon blackstrap molasses

Bring to a boil, stirring occasionally. Reduce the heat and simmer for 5 minutes. Then stir in:

2 cups cooked soybeans

Simmer until the beans are hot. Cool slightly and serve over rice or millet.

yields 4 servings

per serving:

calories 206

protein 15 g

fat 8 g

carb 23 g

fiber 5 g

sodium 255 mg

orange-ginger
garbanzos

Combine in a medium saucepan:

1 cup fresh-squeezed orange juice

2 tablespoons tahini

1 tablespoon tamari

1 tablespoon cornstarch

1 tablespoon grated fresh gingerroot

Whisk or stir well until smooth. Bring to a boil over medium heat, stirring or whisking constantly, then cook at a gentle boil for 1 minute. Stir in:

4 cups cooked garbanzo beans

Cook on low heat until the beans a heated through, about 3 minutes. Cover and remove from the heat. Serve over rice.

yields 4 to 6 servings

per serving:

calories 281

protein 13 g

fat 6 g

carb 45 g

fiber 8 g

sodium 215 mg

barbecue
soybeans

Here's a delicious way to serve soybeans, or you can substitute any other bean of your choice.

In a large skillet, sauté until starting to brown:

  1 cup chopped onions

  3 cloves garlic, minced, or 1 teaspoon garlic powder

  1 teaspoon canola oil

Stir in:

  3 cups water

  1 (6-ounce) can tomato paste

  ⅓ cup brown sugar

  ¼ cup apple cider vinegar

  2 tablespoons tamari

  1 to 2 crushed dried red chili peppers, or 1 to 1½ teaspoons dried red pepper flakes

  1 tablespoon light molasses

  ½ teaspoon ground allspice

  ½ teaspoon salt (optional)

Simmer for 15 minutes, stirring occasionally. Then stir in:

  4 cups cooked soybeans

Simmer for 15 to 20 minutes to let the beans absorb the flavor of the sauce. Serve hot over rice.

yields 8 servings

per serving:

calories 227

protein 16 g

fat 9 g

carb 26 g

fiber 7 g

sodium 314 mg

spicy *lentils*

Combine in a medium saucepan and bring to a boil:

   8 cups water
   2 cups lentils

Reduce the heat, cover, and simmer for 40 minutes. Drain and set aside.

In a large pot, sauté until soft:

   1 large onion, chopped
   1 teaspoon minced garlic
   1 teaspoon olive oil

Stir in:

   1 large tomato, chopped
   1 teaspoon grated fresh gingerroot
   1 teaspoon ground coriander
   1 teaspoon ground cumin
   1 teaspoon ground cardamom
   ½ teaspoon cayenne
   ½ teaspoon salt (optional)

Simmer for 3 minutes. Add the cooked lentils and heat gently until thick. Serve hot over rice.

yields 6 servings

per serving:
calories 133
protein 9 g
fat 1 g
carb 23 g
fiber 9 g
sodium 5 mg

sweet and sour *soybeans*

How can soybeans taste exotic?
Try this recipe and see.

In a medium skillet, sauté until soft:

 1 onion, chopped
 1 cup chopped green peppers
 1 cup chopped celery
 1 clove garlic, minced
 1 teaspoon canola oil

Stir in:

 1 (20-ounce) can unsweetened pineapple chunks (reserve the juice)
 2 cups cooked soybeans

Combine in a jar with a tight fitting lid:

 ¾ cup reserved pineapple juice
 1 tablespoon tamari
 ¼ cup apple cider vinegar
 1½ tablespoons cornstarch
 ¼ teaspoon ground ginger

Shake vigorously until well blended. Pour over the vegetable and bean mixture and simmer until thick, stirring constantly. Gently simmer a few minutes longer. Serve at once over rice.

yields 4 servings

per serving:

calories 285
protein 16 g
fat 9 g
carb 40 g
fiber 7 g
sodium 273 mg

curried
garbanzos

This is a sweet and spicy dish that everyone will enjoy. Leftovers are delicious cold or mashed as a sandwich spread.

Sauté in a large pot until soft:

> 1 large onion, chopped
>
> 3 cloves garlic, minced
>
> 1 teaspoon grated fresh gingerroot
>
> 1 teaspoon canola oil

Stir in:

> 2 medium potatoes, cut into small dice (peeling is optional)
>
> 1 cup fresh or canned chopped tomatoes

Cover and cook for 5 minutes. Then stir in:

> 2 cups cooked garbanzo beans
>
> 1 cup garbanzo stock or water
>
> 1 cup diced tomatoes
>
> 4 tablespoons tomato paste
>
> 2 teaspoons Garam Masala (page 49)
>
> ½ teaspoon salt (optional)
>
> ¼ teaspoon pepper

Stir to combine. Bring to a boil, reduce the heat, and simmer for 10 minutes, stirring occasionally. Serve over rice or millet.

yields 4 to 6 servings

per serving:

calories 204

protein 8 g

fat 3 g

carb 38 g

fiber 7 g

sodium 50 mg

east indian
kidneys

Sauté until tender in a medium skillet:

> 1 cup chopped onions
>
> 1 chili pepper, seeded and minced
>
> 2 large cloves garlic, minced
>
> 1 tablespoon minced or grated fresh gingerroot
>
> 1 teaspoon olive oil

Stir in:

> 1 cup chopped or pureed tomatoes
>
> 1 tablespoon ground coriander
>
> 2 teaspoons Garam Masala (page 49)
>
> 1 teaspoon turmeric
>
> 1 teaspoon ground cumin

Cook for 5 minutes. Then stir in:

> 2½ cups cooked kidney beans
>
> 1 cup bean stock or water

Simmer for 10 minutes, stirring occasionally. Serve hot over rice.

If desired, top with a spoonful of:

> ½ cup nondairy yogurt (optional)

yields 4 servings

per serving:

calories 191

protein 11 g

fat 2 g

carb 34 g

fiber 9 g

sodium 102 mg

curried
limas

This well-seasoned dish contains exotic spices and the sweet taste of apples. It is delightful served over rice or bulgur.

Sauté in a large skillet until brown:

>   1 onion, chopped
>   2 cloves garlic, chopped
>   1 teaspoon canola oil

Stir in:

>   4 cups cooked lima beans
>   2 cups chopped peeled apples (any kind)
>   ½ cup bean stock or water
>   2 tablespoons tamari
>   1 tablespoon fresh lemon juice
>   1 teaspoon paprika
>   1 teaspoon ground coriander
>   1 teaspoon ground cumin
>   ½ teaspoon turmeric
>   ½ teaspoon ground ginger

Cook, stirring occasionally, for 15 minutes or until the apples are tender.

yields 6 servings

per serving:

calories 203
protein 11 g
fat 1 g
carb 38 g
fiber 11 g
sodium 340 mg

coccari's masoor dal
(curried orange lentils)

Combine in a large pot:

> 4½ cups water
> 2 cups orange lentils (masoor dal)
> ½-inch piece fresh gingerroot, grated
> ½ teaspoon salt (optional)
> 1 clove garlic, minced
> ⅛ teaspoon ground coriander
> ⅛ teaspoon ground cumin
> ⅛ teaspoon turmeric

Bring to a boil, lower the heat, and cook until the lentils are very soft, about 30 minutes.

In a small skillet, sauté until brown:

> 1 medium onion, finely chopped
> 2 cloves garlic, minced
> 1-inch piece fresh gingerroot, grated
> 2 teaspoons canola oil

Stir in:

> 1 dried red chili pepper, crushed (optional)
> 1 teaspoon whole cumin seeds
> 1 teaspoon ground coriander
> ¼ teaspoon turmeric
> ⅛ teaspoon Garam Masala (page 49)

yields 6 servings

per serving:

calories 179
protein 12 g
fat 2 g
carb 29 g
fiber 11 g
sodium 4 mg

*This spicy curry dish is quick and
easy to prepare. Serve it with rice,
garnished with fresh coriander
leaves for a special touch.*

Cook about 5 minutes longer, then stir into the cooked lentils and mix well.

Just before serving, stir in:

1 tablespoon fresh lemon juice

Serve warm.

anasazi beans
in miso sauce

Roast in a small skillet until brown and starting to pop:

2 tablespoons sesame seeds

Transfer to a blender or food processor and grind into a powder. Set aside.

Combine in a medium saucepan:

1 cup bean stock or water
2 tablespoons dark miso
1 tablespoon liquid sweetener of your choice
2 cloves garlic, minced

Bring to a simmer and stir until the miso is blended into the stock. Stir in the reserved ground sesame seeds along with:

3 cups cooked Anasazi beans

Cook for 5 to 10 minutes or until hot. Serve over rice or millet.

*yields 4 to 5
servings*

per serving:

calories 267
protein 15 g
fat 3 g
carb 47 g
fiber 10 g
sodium 329 mg

spicy anasazi
beans

Soak overnight:

> 4 cups water
> 1 cup dry Anasazi beans

Drain and add:

> 4 cups fresh water

Bring to a boil, reduce the heat, cover, and simmer until soft, about 1 hour. Drain and set aside.

Sauté in a medium skillet until soft:

> 1 cup chopped onions
> ¾ cup chopped red or green bell peppers
> 2 chili peppers, seeded and minced
> 2 cloves garlic, minced
> 1 teaspoon olive oil

Stir in the cooked and drained Anasazi beans along with:

> 2 cups chopped fresh or canned tomatoes
> 2 tablespoons tomato paste
> 1 teaspoon ground cumin
> 1 teaspoon ground coriander
> 1 teaspoon paprika
> 1 teaspoon turmeric
> ½ teaspoon salt (optional)

Cook for 10 minutes, stirring occasionally. Serve hot over rice.

yields 4 servings

per serving:

calories 241
protein 13 g
fat 2 g
carb 46 g
fiber 10 g
sodium 43 mg

spanish yellow split
peas

Combine in a large pot:

>   6 cups water
>   2 cups dried yellow split peas

Cook until the peas are soft, about 1½ hours. (Soaked peas will cook more quickly.) Drain and set aside.

When the peas are almost finished cooking, sauté for 5 minutes in a large skillet:

>   1 cup diced carrots, diced
>   1 cup chopped onions
>   1 green pepper, chopped
>   3 cloves garlic, minced
>   1 teaspoon olive oil

Stir in:

>   2 cups chopped fresh or canned tomatoes
>   ¼ cup balsamic vinegar
>   2 teaspoons chili powder
>   2 teaspoons ground cumin
>   1 teaspoon dried oregano
>   ½ teaspoon salt (optional)

Mix well. Cover and cook for 10 minutes, stirring occasionally. Add the drained peas and heat for 15 minutes. Serve with rice or a chunk of whole grain bread.

yields 4 to 6 servings

per serving:

calories 142
protein 8 g
fat 2 g
carb 26 g
fiber 9 g
sodium 15 mg

green split pea
curry

Combine in a large pot:

> 6 cups water
> 2 cups (1 pound) dry green split peas

Bring to a boil, reduce the heat, partially cover, and simmer, stirring occasionally, for about 45 minutes. The peas should be tender but still hold their shape.

In a medium skillet, sauté for 1 to 2 minutes:

> 1 tablespoon grated fresh gingerroot
> 1 tablespoon minced garlic
> 1 teaspoon olive oil

Stir in:

> 1 teaspoon brown mustard seeds
> 1 teaspoon whole cumin seeds

Stir while the seeds pop. Then stir in:

> 1 teaspoon Garam Masala (page 49)
> ½ teaspoon salt (optional)

Stir into the cooked split peas and simmer until hot, about 5 minutes. The mixture should be thick. Serve over rice.

yields 4 to 6
servings

per serving:
calories 240
protein 16 g
fat 2 g
carb 42 g
fiber 163 g
sodium 4 mg

more fabulous beans

fruity white *beans*

This is a handy way to incorporate a surplus of apples or pears into the main part of your meal. Serve it over rice or millet.

Combine in a 3-quart pot:

> 2 cups cooked white beans (Great Northern, navy, or limas)
> 2 cups chopped apples or pears, or 1 cup each
> ½ cup chopped onions
> ½ cup bean liquid or water
> 3 to 4 tablespoons fresh lemon juice
> 1½ tablespoon apple cider vinegar
> ½ tablespoon sweetener of your choice
> ½ teaspoon salt (optional)

Cover and simmer, stirring occasionally, for 20 to 25 minutes or until the fruit is quite soft. Remove from the heat and let stand, covered, until ready to serve.

yields 4 servings

per serving:

calories 186
protein 0 g
fat 1 g
carb 38 g
fiber 8 g
sodium 6 mg

marinara lentil
sauce

This sauce is designed to be served over pasta. It also makes a scrumptious sauce for lasagne.

In a deep pot, sauté until tender:

   1 cup chopped onions
   2 cloves garlic, chopped
   1 teaspoon olive oil

Stir in:

   3 cups water
   1¼ cups dry lentils

Bring to a boil, reduce the heat, cover, and simmer for 30 minutes.

Stir in:

   2 cups chopped fresh or canned tomatoes
   2 tablespoons torn fresh basil, or 1/2 teaspoon dried basil
   1 chili pepper, seeded and minced
   ½ teaspoon dried oregano

Cover and simmer for 20 minutes or until the lentils are soft. Then stir in:

   ⅓ cup tomato paste
   ½ to 1 teaspoon salt (optional)

Mix well until the tomato paste is incorporated. Simmer for 15 minutes. Serve hot over pasta.

yields 6 servings

per serving:

calories 158
protein 10 g
fat 2 g
carb 28 g
fiber 10 g
sodium 45 mg

main dishes

pinto bean eggplant *rolls*

Preheat the oven to 350°F. Have ready a 10-inch square baking pan.

Peel and cut lengthways into ¼-inch-thick slices.

> 2 medium eggplants

Steam for 8 to 10 minutes until flexible. Drain in a colander and set aside.

FOR THE FILLING In a large bowl, combine:

> 3 cups cooked pinto beans, mashed
> ⅓ cup wheat germ
> 1 tablespoon chili powder
> 1 teaspoon garlic powder
> 1 teaspoon ground cumin
> ½ teaspoon salt (optional)

Mix well to form a thick paste. Set aside.

FOR THE SAUCE Heat in a medium saucepan:

> 3 cups low-sodium tomato juice or purée
> 1 tablespoon fresh lemon juice
> 1 tablespoon tamari
> 1 teaspoon paprika
> ½ teaspoon dried red pepper flakes (optional)

To assemble the rolls, put a drained eggplant slice on a clean work area. Spoon 2 tablespoons of pinto filling onto the narrow edge of the eggplant. Roll the eggplant around the filling, and place in the reserved baking pan with the rolled edge facing down. When all the rolls are in place, pour the tomato sauce over the top, and bake for 45 minutes.

yields 16 rolls
(6 servings)

per serving:
calories 188
protein 10 g
fat 1 g
carb 365 g
fiber 11 g
sodium 259 mg

crowder pea
pot pie

Preheat the oven to 350°F.

Have ready:

> 1½ cups cooked crowder peas
> 1 (2-quart) straight sided casserole dish or deep-dish pie plate

FOR THE CRUST Combine in a medium bowl:

> 1¼ cups whole wheat pastry flour   3 tablespoons water
> 3 tablespoons canola oil   ½ teaspoon salt (optional)

Mix with a fork, form into a ball, cover, and set aside.

FOR THE GRAVY Combine in a medium saucepan:

> ¼ cup unbleached white flour   ¼ cup nutritional yeast

Toast over medium-low heat, stirring constantly with a wire whisk. Before it gets brown, whisk in:

> 2 cups soymilk   1 tablespoon canola oil

Whisk vigorously to avoid lumps. Stir in:

> 1 teaspoon garlic powder   ½ teaspoon dried thyme
> 1 teaspoon dried sage   ¼ teaspoon pepper
> ½ teaspoon paprika   Salt to taste

Stir until the mixture comes to a boil. Reduce the heat and simmer for 3 minutes, stirring often. Remove from the heat, cover, and set aside.

For the filling: Bring to a boil in a medium saucepan:

> 2 cups water

Crowder peas are a dry pea from the South. They have a pleasant flavor and go perfectly in this dish, which is a variation on a popular regional casserole.

Add:

3 cups peeled and cubed potatoes

Boil for 5 minutes. Then add:

4 cups broccoli florets   1 cup chopped carrots

Reduce the heat, cover, and simmer for 5 minutes. Drain and set aside.

Sauté in a small skillet until tender:

1 onion, chopped   1 teaspoon olive oil

Pour the drained vegetables into the casserole dish. Add the sautéed onion and crowder peas. Pour the gravy over top. Place the reserved dough between two sheets of waxed paper or on a floured surface, and roll it into a circle slightly larger than the top of your casserole dish or pie plate. Carefully place the pie crust over the casserole and pinch the sides to join the edge of the dish. Bake for 35 to 40 minutes. Let cool for 10 minutes before serving.

yields 6 servings

per serving:

calories 375
protein 16 g
fat 13 g
carb 54 g
fiber 11 g
sodium 40 mg

mexican corn and pinto
bean pie

Preheat the oven to 350°F. Oil a 3-quart casserole dish (about 9-inches in diameter) and set aside.

Sauté until tender in a medium skillet:

¾ cup chopped onions

2 cloves garlic, minced

1 teaspoon canola oil

Stir in:

1½ cups chopped fresh or canned tomatoes

1 cup fresh or frozen corn

½ cup chopped green peppers

1 tablespoon chili powder

1 teaspoon ground cumin

Cook 5 minutes, stirring occasionally. Stir in:

3½ cups cooked pinto beans

½ cup chopped black olives

Heat gently while you prepare the topping.

FOR THE TOPPING Combine in a medium bowl:

⅔ cup cornmeal

⅔ cup unbleached white or whole wheat flour

3 tablespoons sugar

1 teaspoon baking powder

¼ teaspoon salt

Make a well in the middle of the dry ingredients, and add:

¾ cup low-fat or regular soymilk   1 tablespoon canola oil

Mix until just combined, but don't beat smooth. Spoon the corn and bean mixture into the prepared casserole dish. Scoop dollops of the corn bread topping over the top and smooth it so it covers most of the bean filling. Bake for 35 minutes.

yields 6 to 8 servings

per serving:

calories 306

protein 11 g

fat 6 g

carb 55 g

fiber 10 g

sodium 219 mg

pinto bean
enchiladas

Preheat the oven to 350°F. Lightly oil a 9 x 13-inch
baking dish and set aside.

Have ready:

10 corn tortillas

FOR THE FILLING Sauté until soft in a heavy skillet:

1 cup chopped onions
3 cloves garlic, minced

½ teaspoon canola oil

Stir in:

4 cups cooked pinto beans
½ cup bean stock or water
2 tablespoons tamari

1 tablespoons tomato paste
1 teaspoon ground cumin

Simmer for 8 to 10 minutes. Remove from the heat and mash the beans with
a fork or potato masher.

FOR THE SAUCE While the bean filling is cooking, sauté until soft in a heavy, 2-
quart saucepan:

½ cup chopped onions
½ cup chopped green peppers

1 tablespoon minced garlic
½ teaspoon canola oil

Stir in:

3 cups low-sodium puréed
tomatoes
2 cups water
3½ tablespoons chili powder

2 teaspoons ground cumin
½ teaspoon dried oregano
½ teaspoon salt (optional)

This dish is easy to prepare, especially if the beans are already cooked. We like it on cool fall evenings, accompanied by a fresh green salad.

Simmer for 10 minutes, stirring occasionally to prevent sticking. Spread 1 cup of the sauce over the bottom of the prepared baking dish. With a pair of tongs, dip a tortilla into the tomato sauce (this keeps the tortilla from cracking when it is folded over) and place it on a plate. Spoon ⅓ cup of the filling in a strip along the center of the tortilla, and wrap the tortilla around the bean filling. Place the enchilada in the baking dish, seam side down. Stuff and roll the remaining tortillas in the same fashion. When all of the tortillas are rolled and in the pan, pour the remaining sauce over the top and bake for 20 to 25 minutes or until bubbly and hot.

yields 6 servings

per serving:

calories 267
protein 12 g
fat 3 g
carb 49 g
fiber 12 g
sodium 364 mg

spicy pinto
casserole

Preheat the oven to 325°F.

Have ready:

- 1 cup crushed baked corn chips
- 1 cup Melted Yeast Cheeze Sauce (next page)

In a heavy-bottomed soup pot, sauté until soft:

- 1 cup chopped onions
- 1 tablespoon minced garlic
- 1 hot chili pepper, seeded and minced,
    or ¼ teaspoon dried red chili flakes or cayenne
- 1 teaspoon canola oil

Stir in:

- 3 cups canned or puréed tomatoes
- 1 cup water
- 1 tablespoon chili powder
- 1 teaspoon dried oregano
- 1 teaspoon ground cumin

Bring to a boil. Then stir in:

- 1 cup dry macaroni or shells
- ½ teaspoon salt (optional)

Simmer for 15 minutes. Stir in:

- 3 cups cooked pinto beans
- 1½ cups fresh, frozen, or canned corn
- ½ cup sliced black olives (optional)

yields 6 servings

per serving:

calories 301
protein 15 g
fat 3 g
carb 57 g
fiber 11 g
sodium 231 mg

Stir until heated throughout. Spoon into a 3-quart casserole dish. Top with the corn chips and Cheeze Sauce, and bake for 15 to 20 minutes or until the Cheeze Sauce begins to brown.

melted yeast cheeze
sauce

This sauce keeps well in the refrigerator if stored in a tightly sealed container. Use it as a cheese spread, a sauce for macaroni, or a topping for pizza.

Combine in a medium saucepan:

> 2 cups water or plain soymilk
> ½ cup nutritional yeast flakes
> 2 tablespoons unbleached white flour
> 2 tablespoons cornstarch
> ½ teaspoon salt (optional)
> ½ teaspoon garlic powder
> ¼ teaspoon turmeric

Cook over medium heat, stirring constantly, until the sauce begins to bubble and thicken. Remove from the heat. While the sauce is still hot, add:

> 1 tablespoon soy margarine
> 2 teaspoons prepared mustard

Stir well and cover until ready for use, or cool and store in the refrigerator. The sauce will thicken considerably as it cools. It may be reheated or used as a cold spread. If the reheated sauce is too thick, add a little water.

yields 2 cups

per ¼ cup:
calories 51
protein 4 g
fat 2 g
carb 6 g
fiber 0.1 g
sodium 31 mg

pinto
pies

Preheat the oven to 350°F.

Combine in a large bowl:

1 cup cooked pinto beans, mashed
1 tomato, finely chopped
1 small onion, minced
¼ cup minced green peppers
2 tablespoons minced fresh parsley
1 tablespoon fresh lemon juice
½ teaspoon garlic powder
½ teaspoon salt (optional)
¼ teaspoon dried basil
¼ teaspoon dried oregano
Pinch of dried red pepper flakes

Mix thoroughly until well blended. Carefully separate into four rounds:

2 whole wheat pita breads

Place the rounds side by side on a cookie sheet. Spread one-fourth of the bean mixture evenly to the edges of each pita round. Bake for 8 to 10 minutes or until the pitas are crisp.

yields 4 pies

per serving:
calories 141
protein 8 g
fat 1 g
carb 26 g
fiber 7 g
sodium 160 mg

lentil
loaf

Preheat the oven to 350°F. Oil a loaf pan and set aside.

Sauté in a small skillet until tender:

> 1 small onion, chopped
> 1 teaspoon olive oil

Transfer the sautéed onions to a bowl and combine with:

> 2 cups cooked lentils
> ½ cup soft bread crumbs
> ½ cup wheat germ
> ½ cup rolled oats
> ½ cup tomato purée
> 2 tablespoons nutritional yeast flakes
> 1 tablespoon apple cider vinegar
> ½ teaspoon dried thyme
> ½ teaspoon salt (optional)

Mix well. Press the mixture into the prepared pan, cover with aluminum foil or a cookie sheet, and bake for 20 minutes. Uncover and bake 10 minutes longer.

yields 4 to 6 servings

per serving:
calories 213
protein 14 g
fat 3 g
carb 35 g
fiber 10 g
sodium 68 mg

navy bean
island loaf

Chill the leftover loaf and slice it to make a delicious sandwich filling.

Preheat the oven to 350°F. Lightly oil a loaf pan and set aside.

Have ready:

> 1 (16-ounce) can crushed pineapple, drained (reserve juice)

In a blender, grind into a coarse meal:

> ⅓ cup sunflower seeds

Transfer to a large bowl and combine with:

> 3 cups cooked navy beans, mashed
> 1 cup soft whole wheat bread crumbs
> 1 green pepper, chopped
> ½ cup rolled oats
> ⅓ cup reserved pineapple juice
> 1 tablespoon light molasses
> 1 tablespoon prepared spicy mustard
> ½ teaspoon garlic powder
> ½ teaspoon salt (optional)

Mix well and press into the prepared loaf pan.

Spread the crushed pineapple over the top of the loaf, and bake for 45 minutes.

yields 6 servings

per serving:

calories 278
protein 12 g
fat 6 g
carb 48 g
fiber 8 g
sodium 64 mg

garbanzo-vegetable *loaf*

This tasty loaf is a treat with mashed potatoes and gravy and a leafy green salad. Enjoy it sliced in a sandwich, if you have any leftovers.

Preheat the oven to 350°F. Lightly oil a loaf pan and set aside.

Heat in a skillet:

Sauté in a medium skillet until tender:

> 1½ cups grated carrots
>
> 1½ cups finely chopped celery
>
> 1 cup chopped onions
>
> 3 cloves garlic, minced
>
> 1 teaspoon olive oil

Transfer to a large bowl and combine with:

> 3½ cups cooked garbanzo beans, mashed
>
> 1 cup soft whole wheat bread crumbs
>
> ½ cup apple juice
>
> ¼ cup minced fresh parsley
>
> 1 tablespoon dried tarragon
>
> ¼ teaspoon dried thyme
>
> ½ teaspoon dried savory
>
> ½ teaspoon salt (optional)

Spoon the mixture into the prepared loaf pan, cover with aluminum foil, and bake for 1 hour. Cool the loaf in the pan before removing.

yields 6 servings

per serving:

calories 223

protein 10 g

fat 4 g

carb 38 g

fiber 8 g

sodium 80 mg

garbanzo stuffed
acorn squash

Preheat the oven to 350°F. Have ready a 9 x 13-inch baking dish.

Cut in half lengthways:

> 3 acorn squash

Remove the seeds and pulp with a spoon. Poke the outside skin of each piece with a fork to let the steam penetrate. Fill a large pot with ½ inch of water, add the squash, cover, and bring to a boil. Reduce the heat and steam for 15 minutes. Uncover and set aside.

FOR THE TOMATO SAUCE Combine in a saucepan and heat over medium until hot:

> 2 cups chopped tomatoes
> ¼ cup tomato paste
>
> ¼ cup fresh lemon juice
> ½ teaspoon garlic powder

In a large skillet, sauté until soft:

> 1½ cups chopped onions
> 2 cloves garlic, minced
>
> 1 teaspoon olive oil

Stir in:

> 1 cup chopped fresh or canned tomatoes or tomato purée
> 1 tablespoon tomato paste
> 1½ cups cooked brown or white rice
>
> 1½ cups cooked garbanzo beans
> ½ teaspoon ground cinnamon
> ¼ teaspoon ground cloves
> 1 teaspoon salt (optional)

Mix well and cook until hot.

To assemble, stuff each squash half with one-sixth of the filling, and place in the reserved baking dish. Pour the tomato sauce over the squash, cover with aluminum foil, and bake for 30 minutes.

yields 6 servings

per serving:

calories 232
protein 8 g
fat 3 g
carb 48 g
fiber 11 g
sodium 55 mg

noodle, veggie, and soybean
casserole

Be creative with this dish; use whatever vegetables you have on hand.

Preheat the oven to 350°F. Lightly oil a 3-quart casserole dish and set aside. Have ready:

2 cups cooked whole wheat noodles

1 cup cooked soybeans

¼ cup minced fresh parsley

1 tomato, sliced

Sauté in a medium skillet until lightly browned:

1 cup chopped celery

¾ cup chopped onions

1 teaspoon canola oil

Stir in until evenly blended:

3 tablespoons whole wheat flour

Stir constantly while gradually adding:

1½ cups soybean stock or water

Bring to a boil, stirring constantly, until the sauce thickens.

Stir in:

1 carrot, grated

1 tomato, chopped

1 cup fresh or frozen corn

½ teaspoon dried tarragon

¼ teaspoon dried sage

¼ teaspoon dried thyme

½ teaspoon salt (optional)

⅛ teaspoon pepper

Simmer for 3 minutes. Stir the soybeans and cooked noodles into the vegetable sauce, and spoon the mixture into the prepared casserole dish. Arrange the sliced tomato on top of the casserole and sprinkle with the parsley. Bake for 20 to 25 minutes or until bubbly and hot.

yields 4 to 5 servings

per serving:

calories 262

protein 14 g

fat 6 g

carb 44 g

fiber 10 g

sodium 46 mg

garbanzo
moussaka

Preheat the oven to 350°F.

Lightly oil a 9 x 13-inch baking pan and set aside.

Have ready:

> 2 medium eggplants
> salt

Slice the eggplants into ¼-inch rounds, sprinkle with salt, and let sit in a colander in the sink while you prepare the filling and white sauce. The salt will draw out some of the bitterness from the eggplants.

FOR THE BEAN FILLING Sauté in a medium skillet until beginning to brown:

> 1 cup chopped onions
> 2 cloves garlic, minced
> 1 teaspoon olive oil

Stir in:

> 2 cups cooked garbanzo beans, mashed
> 2 cups tomato purée
> ¼ cup chopped fresh parsley
> 2 tablespoons fresh lemon juice
> ½ teaspoon ground cinnamon
> ½ teaspoon salt (optional)
> ⅛ teaspoon pepper

Cook over low heat, stirring occasionally, for 15 minutes.

This Greek casserole is ideal for busy schedules. You can assemble it and store it in the refrigerator, then bake it whenever you wish.

FOR THE WHITE SAUCE Combine in a small saucepan and whisk together until smooth:

2 cups low-fat or regular soymilk   ¼ cup unbleached white flour
½ cup nutritional yeast flakes

Heat over medium, stirring occasionally with the whisk. When the sauce thickens, add:

1 tablespoon soy margarine   ½ teaspoon salt

Stir well, remove from the heat, cover, and set aside.

Rinse the eggplant slices to remove the salt and pat the rounds dry.

To assemble the casserole, layer the eggplant and half of the bean filling in the prepared baking pan. Repeat, ending with a layer of eggplant. Pour the white sauce evenly over the casserole. If desired, sprinkle the top with:

½ cup bread crumbs (optional)

Bake for 35 to 45 minutes. Cool for 10 minutes before cutting into squares.

yields 6 servings

per serving:
calories 262
protein 15 g
fat 6 g
carb 42 g
fiber 8 g
sodium 183 mg

stuffed cabbage
with black-eyed peas

Preheat the oven to 350°F. Have ready a 9 x 13-inch baking dish.

FOR THE FILLING In a medium skillet, sauté until soft:

> 1 cup chopped onions
> 1 cup chopped celery stalks and leaves
> 3 cloves garlic, minced
> 2 chili peppers, seeded minced (optional)
> 1 teaspoon olive oil

Stir in:

> 2 cups cooked black-eyed peas
> 2 cups cooked brown rice
> 1 teaspoon ground cumin
> 1 teaspoon ground coriander

Mix well and cook gently for 5 to 10 minutes to let the flavors blend. Set aside.

Bring to a boil in a large covered pot:

> 2 cups water

Meanwhile, core:

> 1 large head cabbage

Carefully peel off 10 to 12 of the large outer leaves without tearing them. Place them in the boiling water and steam for 5 minutes to soften. Save the water. Chop the smaller leaves and any larger, split leaves and place 2 cups of them on the bottom of the baking dish.

This stuffed cabbage is an interesting version of an old favorite.

To make the sauce, combine in a medium pot:

- 3 cups tomato purée
- 2 cups low-sodium spaghetti sauce
- 2 tablespoons fresh lemon juice
- 1 teaspoon garlic powder
- 1 teaspoon dried basil

Simmer for 10 minutes and set aside.

Pour ½ cup of the cabbage liquid over the chopped cabbage in the casserole dish. Put a steamed cabbage leaf on a clean work area. If it is too stiff to roll, cut out a V-shaped section of the core end of the cabbage. Spoon about ⅓ cup of filling onto the center of the cabbage leaf. Fold over two sides of the leaf and, starting with the core end, firmly roll the cabbage over the filling. If the cabbage leaf doesn't overlap, remove some of the filling and roll again.

Place the cabbage roll seam side down over the cabbage in the baking dish. Roll up all of the steamed leaves in a similar fashion until the baking dish is full. Pour the tomato sauce over all, and bake for 35 minutes.

yields 6 servings

per serving:

calories 275
protein 12 g
fat 4 g
carb 51 g
fiber 12 g
sodium 235 mg

soy stuffed
peppers

Preheat the oven to 350°F. Have ready a shallow 9 x 13-inch baking pan.

Have ready:

> 2 cups spaghetti sauce

Cut in half lengthwise:

> 4 large green or red bell peppers

Remove the stems and seeds and place the peppers in a deep pan. Cover with boiling water. Cover the pan with foil and let stand while preparing the filling.

FOR THE FILLING In a large pot, sauté until soft:

> 1 cup shredded carrots
>
> 1 cup chopped onions
>
> ½ cup chopped celery
>
> 1 teaspoon canola oil

Stir in:

> 2 cups cooked soybeans
>
> 2 cups cooked brown rice or millet
>
> 1 cup chopped tomatoes
>
> ¼ cup chopped fresh parsley
>
> ½ teaspoon salt (optional)
>
> ½ teaspoon garlic powder
>
> ¼ teaspoon dried thyme
>
> ¼ teaspoon dried basil
>
> ¼ teaspoon pepper

Stir and cook on low heat for 5 minutes.

Remove the peppers from the water, stuff each half with several heaping tablespoons of the filling, and place them in the reserved pan. Pour the spaghetti sauce around (not over) the peppers.

FOR THE TOPPING Combine in a small bowl:

2 tablespoons nutritional yeast flakes   2 tablespoons wheat germ

Sprinkle the topping over the peppers and bake for 40 minutes.

yields 6 servings

per serving:

calories 280
protein 16 g
fat 7 g
carb 402 g
fiber 9 g
sodium 224 mg

black bean tamale
stuffed peppers

Preheat the oven to 350°F. Have ready a shallow baking dish large enough to hold 6 bell peppers standing upright.

Slice off the tops and remove the seeds from:

6 green or red bell peppers

Fill a large pot partway with water and bring to a boil. Blanch the peppers for 5 minutes. Drain and set aside.

In a medium skillet, sauté until soft:

1 cup chopped onions
3 cloves garlic, minced

1 teaspoon canola oil

Stir in:

3 cups chopped tomatoes
¾ cup yellow cornmeal
1½ tablespoons chili powder

1½ teaspoons cumin
½ teaspoon salt (optional)

Mix well and cook, stirring constantly, until thick. Then stir in:

2 cups cooked black beans
1½ cups frozen corn

Cook until hot. Fill each steamed pepper with one-sixth of the filling. Place the stuffed peppers upright in the reserved baking dish, pour ½ inch of water into the baking dish, and bake for 25 minutes.

yields 6 servings

per serving:

calories 221
protein 9 g
fat 2 g
carb 45 g
fiber 10 g
sodium 19 mg

lima bean
succotash

When I was a child, we enjoyed this dish when the lima beans were fresh from the garden. It's equally delicious using dry lima beans.

Preheat the oven to 350°F. Oil a 2- to 3-quart casserole dish and set aside.

In a large skillet, sauté until tender:

> 1 onion, chopped
> ¾ cup chopped celery
> 1 clove garlic, minced
> 1 teaspoon olive oil

In a small bowl, whisk until smooth:

> 1 cup bean stock or water
> 3 tablespoons unbleached white flour
> 1 tablespoon tamari

Pour over the onion and celery, whisking to form a smooth sauce. Then stir in:

> 2½ cups fresh or frozen corn
> 2 cups cooked lima beans
> ⅔ cup plain soymilk
> ⅛ teaspoon grated nutmeg

Bring to a boil, stirring constantly. Pour into the prepared casserole dish and bake for 20 to 25 minutes.

yields 5 to 6 servings

per serving:

calories 175
protein 9 g
fat 2 g
carb 34 g
fiber 8 g
sodium 190 mg

black-eyed
spirals

FOR THE DOUGH Dissolve in a medium bowl:

> 1½ cups lukewarm water
> 2 tablespoons sweetener of your choice
> 1 package (1 tablespoon) dry baker's yeast

Whisk in:

> 1 cup unbleached white flour

Let sit until bubbly, about 10 minutes. Then beat in using a wooden spoon:

> 1½ cups unbleached white flour
> 1½ cups whole wheat flour
> ¼ cup wheat germ
> 1 tablespoon canola oil
> ¼ teaspoon salt

Knead on a lightly floured surface for 5 minutes or until smooth. Add more flour if the dough is too sticky, but keep the dough soft and satiny. Transfer it to a lightly oiled bowl, cover with a damp cloth, and prepare the filling.

Preheat the oven to 350°F. Lightly oil a cookie sheet and set aside.

FOR THE FILLING Soak for 10 to 15 minutes:

> 1 cup dried tomatoes
> ½ cup boiling water

This is an easy, quick-dough recipe filled with tasty beans and vegetables. These rolls are great served warm for supper but they also make tasty picnic or lunch fare.

Drain. Transfer to a large bowl or a food processor (for a smoother consistency) along with:

3 cups cooked black-eyed peas, mashed

3 cups well-drained, chopped cooked spinach, collards, or kale

½ cup chopped fresh parsley

¼ cup fresh lemon juice

2 tablespoons (5 to 6 cloves) minced garlic

2 tablespoons tamari

2 teaspoons dried dill weed

Stir with a fork or process until well combined.

Roll out the dough on a lightly floured surface into a 15-inch square, about ¼-inch thick. Spread the filling to cover the surface, leaving a ½-inch margin around the edges. Starting with one edge, roll the dough around the filling as if you were making cinnamon rolls. This will make one large log. With a sharp knife, cut the log into 1-inch pieces, and place the pieces on their side on the prepared cookie sheet so the spirals are facing up. If any of the spirals unravel a bit, just pinch the dough back together. Bake for 20 to 25 minutes.

yields 12 to 14 spirals

per spiral :

calories 222

protein 9 g

fat 2 g

carb 44 g

fiber 7 g

sodium 290 mg

lentils
and eggplant

Serve this sweet and sour lentil sauce over rice, millet, or couscous.

Combine in a medium saucepan:

3 cups water   1 cup dry lentils

Bring to a boil, reduce the heat, cover, and simmer for 30 minutes. Drain and set aside.

Place in a medium bowl:

1 medium eggplant, cubed (peeling is optional)

Sprinkle with:

½ cup whole wheat flour

Toss until the eggplant cubes are evenly coated.

Heat in a large skillet:

1 teaspoon olive oil

When hot, add the coated eggplant and:

1 cup thinly sliced onion crescents

Cook and stir until the eggplant is evenly browned. Then add:

1½ cups low-sodium tomato juice or tomato purée
2 tablespoons tamari
2 tablespoons apple cider vinegar
1 tablespoons sweetener of your choice
1 teaspoon chili powder
½ teaspoon garlic powder

Mix well and simmer for 15 minutes. Add the drained lentils, cover, and cook on low for 20 minutes or until the lentils are quite soft.

yields 5 servings

per serving:

calories 214
protein 12 g
fat 2 g
carb 40 g
fiber 11 g
sodium 258 mg

more fabulous beans

tanzanian kidneys
with coconut

Fresh coconut is best for this dish, but you can use dried if fresh isn't available.

Boil until tender but not mushy:

> 2 cups peeled and cubed potatoes

Set aside.

In a large skillet, sauté for 1 to 2 minutes::

> 3 cloves garlic, minced
> ½ teaspoon canola oil

Stir in:

> ½ cup bean stock or water
> ½ cup grated fresh coconut or dried unsweetened coconut
> juice of 1 lime (about 1 to 2 tablespoons)
> 2 teaspoons ground coriander
> 2 teaspoons ground cumin
> 2 teaspoons turmeric
> 1 chili pepper, seeded and minced, or ¾ teaspoon dried red pepper flakes
> ½ teaspoon salt (optional)

Cook over medium heat until bubbly. Stir in the reserved cooked potatoes and:

> 5 cups cooked kidney beans

Cover and cook over low heat for several minutes until heated through. Serve hot over rice.

yields 6 servings

per serving:

calories 363
protein 15 g
fat 13 g
carb 50 g
fiber 14 g
sodium 13 mg

bean sprout
curry

Here is a delicious curry that will go beautifully with your favorite Indian dal or a tossed salad and rice.

In a large skillet, sauté for 5 minutes::

    ¾ cup chopped onions
    1 clove garlic, minced
    1 teaspoon grated fresh gingerroot
    1 teaspoon olive oil

Stir in:

    3 medium potatoes, cut into ½-inch dice (peeling is optional)
    ¾ cup fresh or canned chopped tomatoes
    ½ cup water

Cover and cook over medium heat for 10 to 15 minutes or until the potatoes are almost soft. Then stir in:

    2½ cups mung bean or lentil sprouts (see page 50)
    1½ teaspoons Garam Masala (page 49)
    ½ teaspoon salt (optional)
    ¼ teaspoon pepper

Cover and simmer 2 to 3 minutes or until the sprouts are wilted but not soft. Serve at once over rice.

yields 4 to 6 servings

per serving:

calories 109
protein 4 g
fat 1 g
carb 23 g
fiber 3 g
sodium 10 mg

soybean
stroganoff

This is so easy to prepare. Serve it with a fresh green salad and your choice of pasta for a tasty dinner.

In a medium skillet, sauté until soft:

> 2½ cups (8 ounces) chopped fresh mushrooms
> 1 cup diced onions
> ½ teaspoon olive oil

In a small bowl or cup, combine:

> 2 tablespoons tamari
> 1 tablespoon cornstarch
> ⅛ teaspoon pepper

Mix until the cornstarch is dissolved and then stir the paste into the mushrooms and onions. Mix well and cook and stir until the sauce is bubbly and smooth. Stir in:

> 2 cups cooked soybeans
> 1 cup soymilk or plain soy yogurt

Simmer gently until warmed through. Do not boil or the sauce may separate and curdle. Serve at once over pasta.

yields 4 servings

per serving:

calories 213
protein 18 g
fat 10 g
carb 17 g
fiber 7 g
sodium 514 mg

navy bean balls
with mushroom gravy

Combine in a bowl:

> 1 cup fresh or soft whole wheat breadcrumbs
> ½ cup wheat germ
> ½ cup plain soymilk

Mix well and let rest to allow the breadcrumbs to absorb the soymilk.

Mash in a food processor:

> 3 cups cooked navy beans

Transfer to a bowl and stir in:

> 1 small onion, minced
> ½ teaspoon salt (optional)
> ¼ teaspoon ground coriander

Squeeze any excess liquid from the soaked breadcrumbs (reserve the liquid for the gravy) and add to the bean mixture. Mix thoroughly and shape into 1-inch balls. Place in a vegetable steamer (they'll expand a little bit), cover, and steam for 10 minutes. Remove from the heat and let rest, covered, for 5 minutes before serving.

mushroom gravy

Combine in a saucepan:

> 1 cup chopped mushrooms
> 2 tablespoons water

Cook until the mushrooms are softened.

Stir with a fork:

> 1½ cups plain soymilk, or ¾ cup plain soymilk and ¾ cup water
> 3 tablespoons cornstarch

Pour into the mushrooms while stirring with a wire whisk to avoid lumps. Then whisk in:

> 2 tablespoons tamari
> ¼ teaspoon garlic powder

Continue to whisk until the sauce thickens and begins to bubble. Serve over the bean balls.

yields 6 servings

per serving:

calories 232
protein 14 g
fat 4 g
carb 38 g
fiber 8 g
sodium 374 mg

baby limas
armenian

This bean dish is intended to be an accompaniment to a large meal. It's also a good dish for a potluck.

Soak overnight or use the quick-soak method (see page 9):

   1 cup dried baby lima beans, or 2 cups canned lima beans

Drain, transfer to a large pot, and add:

   3 cups water

Bring to a boil, lower the heat, cover, and simmer for 30 to 35 minutes or until tender.

Meanwhile, sauté in a small skillet until tender:

   1 carrot, thinly sliced
   1 stalk celery, chopped
   1 clove garlic, minced
   ½ teaspoon olive oil

Stir into the cooked beans along with:

   2 tablespoons chopped fresh parsley
   1 tablespoon minced fresh dill weed, or 1 teaspoon dried dill weed
   ½ teaspoon salt (optional)
   ¼ teaspoon pepper

Cover and keep warm until ready to serve.

yields 4 to 6 servings

per serving:

calories 105
protein 6 g
fat 1 g
carb 19 g
fiber 6 g
sodium 15 mg

summer cannelloni
and veggies

Cornbread goes well with this hearty, stew-like mélange of vegetables and beans. You can omit the cauliflower and zucchini for a quicker meal. Pictured on the cover.

In a large skillet, sauté until tender but not mushy:

  2 cups cauliflower, broken into bite-size florets
  2 cups fresh green beans, cut into 1-inch pieces
  1½ cups chopped fresh or canned tomatoes
  ½ cup tomato puree
  1 onion, chopped
  1 medium zucchini, chopped
  1 teaspoon olive oil

Stir in:

  2 cups cooked cannelloni or white beans
  2 tablespoons chopped fresh parsley
  1 tablespoon chopped fresh basil, or 1 teaspoon dried basil
  1 tablespoon dried dill weed, crushed
  salt to taste

Mix well and heat until warmed through. Serve hot.

yields 6 servings

per serving:
calories 143
protein 9 g
fat 1 g
carb 27 g
fiber 8 g
sodium 55 mg

ceci all' italiana
italian garbanzos

Cook in boiling water until tender:

> 2 cups (½ pound) uncooked shells, spirals, or elbows

Drain and set aside in a covered pot to keep hot while preparing the garbanzo sauce.

In a large skillet, sauté for 3 to 5 minutes:

> 1 head of cauliflower, broken into bite-size flowerets, or 1 (10-ounce)
>   package frozen cauliflower
> 1 onion, chopped
> 2 cloves garlic, minced
> ⅛ teaspoon dried red pepper flakes
> 1 teaspoon olive oil

Stir in:

> 4 cups fresh or canned chopped tomatoes
> 2 cups cooked garbanzo beans
> ¾ cup chopped black olives (optional)
> ¼ cup chopped fresh parsley
> 1 tablespoon balsamic vinegar
> 1 teaspoon dried oregano
> 1 teaspoon dried basil
> 1 teaspoon salt (optional)

Cover and simmer until the cauliflower is soft. Pour the sauce over the pasta, mix well, and serve immediately.

yields 6 servings

per serving:

calories 274
protein 12 g
fat 3 g
carb 52 g
fiber 7 g
sodium 32 mg

more fabulous beans

black-eyed peas
with greens

Sauté until tender in a medium skillet:

> 1 onion, chopped
>
> 1 small chili pepper, seeded and minced, or 1/4 teaspoon cayenne
>
> 1 teaspoon olive oil

Stir in:

> 5 cups cooked black-eyed peas
>
> 4 cups chopped greens (spinach, beet greens, or kale)
>
> 1 cup bean stock or water
>
> ½ cup raisins
>
> 1 tablespoon tamari
>
> ¼ teaspoon ground allspice

Cover and cook, stirring occasionally, for 5 to 10 minutes or until the greens are tender. Serve over rice.

yields 6 servings

per serving:

calories 229

protein 13 g

fat 2 g

carb 43 g

fiber 12 g

sodium 207 mg

lima combo

over couscous

This colorful dish is quick to prepare and has an extraordinary flavor.

Sauté until tender in a large skillet:

> 1 cup chopped onions
> 1 bell pepper, chopped
> 1 cup diced carrots
> 1 teaspoon olive oil

Stir in:

> 2 cups cooked lima beans
> 2 cups chopped fresh or canned tomatoes
> 2 cups diced zucchini
> 1 cup fresh or frozen green peas
> 1 teaspoon whole fennel seeds

Simmer for 10 minutes. Then add:

> 1 cup sliced mushrooms
> ¼ cup raisins
> ½ teaspoon salt (optional)
> ⅛ teaspoon dried red pepper flakes (optional)

Mix well and simmer for 10 minutes.

Meanwhile, combine in a medium serving bowl:

> 3 cups boiling water
> 1½ cups couscous

Mix well. Cover and let stand for 10 minutes. Uncover and fluff with a fork. Transfer the couscous to a serving platter. Ladle the lima bean sauce over the couscous and serve.

yields 6 servings

per serving:

calories 264
protein 12 g
fat 2 g
carb 53 g
fiber 10 g
sodium 24 mg

more fabulous beans

diane's eggplant curry
and black-eyed peas

Heat in a medium skillet:

> 1 tablespoon canola oil

When hot, add:

> 2 dried red chili peppers, crushed
>
> ½ teaspoon brown mustard seeds

Cook until the mustard seeds begin to pop. Stir in:

> 1 cup dry black-eyed peas, soaked overnight or 1 (10-ounce) package
>   frozen black-eyed peas
>
> enough water to cover the peas
>
> ½ teaspoon salt (optional)
>
> ¼ teaspoon turmeric

Bring to a boil, reduce the heat, cover, and simmer until the peas are tender. (Frozen peas will cook faster than soaked peas.) Then stir in:

> 2 medium, unpeeled eggplants, cut into small cubes
>
> 1 small onion, chopped
>
> ¼ cup water
>
> 1 teaspoon grated fresh gingerroot

Cover and cook over low heat for 15 minutes. Stir in:

> 2 tablespoons chopped fresh cilantro

Remove from the heat and let stand, covered, for 5 to 10 minutes before serving.

My sister-in-law Diane, who inspired this recipe, lived in Varanasi, India for a while and got a feel for Indian spices and cooking. This can be either a side dish or the focus of a meal, accompanied by salad and rice.

yields 4 to 6
servings

per serving:
calories 131
protein 6 g
fat 3 g
carb 20 g
fiber 7 g
sodium 5 mg

butternut aduki
skillet

Sauté in a medium skillet for 1 to 2 minutes:

> 2 tablespoons minced garlic
> 1 teaspoon olive oil

Push the garlic to the side of the skillet and add:

> 3 cups peeled and cubed butternut squash
> ⅓ cup water

Cover and cook for 5 to 7 minutes or until the squash is tender but still firm. Stir in:

> 2 cups cooked aduki beans
> ¼ cup chopped fresh cilantro

Cook over medium heat for a few minutes until the beans are hot. Cover, remove from the heat, and let rest for several minutes to allow the flavors to blend.

yields 5 servings

per serving:

calories 185
protein 8 g
fat 1 g
carb 38 g
fiber 9 g
sodium 13 mg

caribbean black-eyed pea
stir-fry

Sauté for 3 to 5 minutes in a large skillet:

> 1½ cups chopped onions
> 1 green bell pepper, chopped
> 1 cup diced celery
> 1 cup diced carrots
> 1 cup fresh or frozen green peas
> ¾ cup raw cashews
> 1 teaspoon olive oil

Stir in:

> 3 cups cooked black-eyed peas
> 2 cups cooked brown rice
> 1 cup pineapple tidbits (reserve juice)
> ¼ cup pineapple juice (from the tidbits)
> 2 tablespoons tamari

Mix well and simmer until hot.

yields 6 to 8 servings

per serving:

calories 313
protein 12 g
fat 9 g
carb 48 g
fiber 9 g
sodium 318 mg

brazilian
black beans

This combination of black beans, Spanish rice, kale, and marinated onions is derived from traditional Brazilian cuisine. It's a complete meal served on a platter from which individual servings are taken.

Combine in a small bowl:

    1½ medium onions, sliced into thin rounds
juice of 2 limes (2 to 4 tablespoons)
1 teaspoon hot red pepper sauce

Set aside to marinate.

Combine in a medium pot:

2 cups brown rice	2 cups tomato juice
2 cups water	1 bay leaf

Bring to a boil, reduce the heat, and simmer for 30 to 40 minutes or until the rice is tender. Remove from the heat and let stand, covered, for 10 minutes.

In a soup pot sauté until soft:

1 onion, chopped	3 cloves garlic, minced
2 to 3 jalapeño peppers, seeded and minced	1 teaspoon olive oil

Stir in and simmer until hot:

5 cups cooked black beans	2 cups chopped fresh or canned tomatoes

Steam until tender:

    2 to 3 quarts chopped fresh kale

To serve, put a flat mound of rice in the center of a large platter. Scoop the black bean sauce over the rice. Arrange the steamed kale around the rice. Arrange the marinated onion rings over all, and pour the lime marinade over the entire platter.

yields 6 to 8 servings

per serving:
calories 369
protein 17 g
fat 3 g
carb 72 g
fiber 15 g
sodium 93 mg

anasazi beans
and rice

What an easy recipe, you say? True, but taste these pretty beans, and you'll see why they don't need a lot of extra flavorings. Try them plain or served with your favorite chutney or relish.

Soak overnight or use the quick-soak method (see page 9)

> 4 cups water
> 1 cup dry Anasazi beans

Drain and add:

> 3 cups fresh water
> 1 bay leaf

Bring to a boil and simmer for 10 minutes. Stir in:

> 1 cup brown rice
> 1 clove garlic, coarsely chopped
> 1 jalapeño pepper, seeded and chopped
> 1 tablespoon tamari

Cover and simmer gently for 40 minutes.

yields 4 to 6
servings

per serving:

calories 237
protein 11 g
fat 1 g
carb 47 g
fiber 7 g
sodium 214 mg

lentils
and rice

Lentils and rice, both so chewy and hearty, are a natural combination. This dish is very easy to prepare. It lets you concentrate on putting together a fresh tossed salad to accompany your meal.

Combine in a 3-quart saucepan:

  6 cups water
  2 cups dry lentils
  1 cup brown rice

Bring to a boil, lower the heat, cover, and simmer for 40 minutes.

In a medium skillet, sauté until soft and transparent:

  1 cup chopped onions
  2 cloves garlic, minced
  1 teaspoon olive oil

Stir into the cooked lentils and rice along with:

  1 tablespoon tamari
  1 teaspoon ground cumin
  1 teaspoon ground coriander
  ¼ teaspoon pepper

Cook for 10 minutes, remove from the heat, and let rest, covered, for 5 to 10 minutes. Just before serving, drizzle over each portion:

  3 to 4 tablespoons fresh lemon juice

yields 6 servings

per serving:

calories 248
protein 14 g
fat 2 g
carb 45 g
fiber 12 g
sodium 174 mg

hoppin' john
with black-eyed peas

This dish is traditionally served with corn bread on New Year's Day to ensure good health and prosperity for the year ahead. There is no need to enjoy it only once a year.

Soak overnight or for four hours:

  4 cups water
  1 cup black-eyed peas

Drain. Transfer to a soup pot and add:

  4 cups vegetable broth or water
  ⅔ cup brown rice
  ½ cup dried tomatoes
  1 teaspoon dried red pepper flakes

Bring to a boil, reduce the heat, cover, and simmer for 45 minutes.

In a large skillet, sauté until tender:

  1 onion, chopped
  5 cloves garlic, minced
  ½ teaspoon olive oil

Stir into the cooked peas and rice and add:

  ½ cup chopped fresh parsley
  2 tablespoons balsamic vinegar
  salt to taste

Simmer uncovered for 5 minutes.

yields 6 servings

per serving:
calories 187
protein 8 g
fat 2 g
carb 36 g
fiber 7 g
sodium 104 mg

curried split peas
with rice

You may have to go to an international market to find Indian pickles or curry paste, but it will be worth the trip. The flavors of this dish are irresistible. The yogurt topping is a welcome contrast to the heat of the peas and rice.

Have ready:

> 3 cups cooked brown or white rice (keep hot)

Combine in a small bowl:

> 1 cup plain nondairy yogurt
> ½ teaspoon ground coriander

> ½ teaspoon ground cumin
> ¼ teaspoon ground cardamom

Mix well, cover, and keep in the refrigerator until ready to serve.

Combine in a heavy-bottomed pan:

> 4½ cups water
> 1 cup dry split peas

Bring to a boil, reduce the heat, partially cover, and simmer for 30 minutes.

Stir in:

> 3½ cups peeled and cubed sweet potatoes

Partially cover and simmer for 10 minutes, stirring occasionally.

Sauté until soft in a small skillet:

> 1 onion, chopped
> 1 red bell pepper, sliced into thin strips
> 2 tablespoons minced garlic
> 1 teaspoon olive oil

Add the pea and sweet potatoes along with:

> ¼ cup Indian pickles or curry paste (if using pickles, sliver the chunks)

Stir well and simmer for 5 to 10 minutes. Remove from the heat, cover, and let rest until ready to serve. Serve over the hot rice with a large spoonful of the yogurt topping.

yields 6 servings

per serving:

calories 345
protein 13 g
fat 3 g
carb 69 g
fiber 13 g
sodium 229 mg

white bean
tzimmes

Tzimmes is a Jewish dish which is traditionally prepared for the Passover meal. This variation is good any time of year.

Combine in a 3-quart pot:

> 5 cups water
> 1 cup dry white beans

Bring to a boil, reduce the heat, cover, and simmer for 30 minutes. Stir in:

> ½ cup brown rice
> 2 cups chunked carrots (in 1-inch pieces)
> 2 cups peeled and diced sweet potatoes
> 1 cup halved pitted prunes
> 1 cup chopped onions

Cover and simmer for 30 minutes. Stir in:

> 3 to 4 tablespoons fresh lemon juice
> 2 tablespoons sweetener of your choice
> ½ teaspoon salt (optional)

Cook and stir for 15 to 20 minutes longer until everything is soft and the tzimmes is thick.

yields 6 servings

per serving:

calories 301
protein 10 g
fat 1 g
carb 66 g
fiber 11 g
sodium 24 mg

black beans
and noodles

Cook in lightly salted boiling water until al dente:

> 2 cups (½ pound) whole wheat pasta

Drain, rinse, drain again, and set aside.

In a large skillet, sauté for 5 minutes or until soft:

> 2½ cups shredded cabbage
> 1 cup celery, chopped
> 4 to 5 scallions, chopped
> 2 cloves garlic, minced
> 1 teaspoon canola oil

Stir in:

> 2 tablespoons tamari
> 1 tablespoon minced fresh cilantro

Add the reserved pasta along with:

> 2½ cups cooked black beans

Mix well. Cover and simmer for a few minutes to allow the flavors to blend. Serve hot.

yields 6 servings

per serving:

calories 258
protein 14 g
fat 2 g
carb 50 g
fiber 124 g
sodium 358 mg

garbanzo
manicotti

*Enjoy this manicotti
with a special twist.
Using a pastry bag
with its tip removed
to fill the pasta
makes this dish a
breeze to prepare.*

Preheat the oven to 375°F. Have ready a 9 x 13-inch glass baking dish.

Boil until al denté:

14 manicotti shells

Drain and set aside.

Sauté in a small skillet until light brown:

1 onion, chopped
6 cloves of garlic, chopped
1 teaspoon olive oil

Transfer them to a food processor along with:

3 cups cooked garbanzo beans
1 (15.5-ounce) jar roasted red peppers, drained (1¾ cups)
¼ cup raw cashews
⅓ cup rolled oats
2 tablespoons tomato paste
1 teaspoon dried oregano

Process until blended but not completely smooth to give the mixture some
texture. Spoon into a pastry bag with no tip attached or use a gallon
plastic bag with a corner cut off if you don't have a pastry bag. Fill the
manicotti shells and place them in the baking dish. Cover with:

1 (26-ounce) jar pasta sauce (3 cups)

Bake for 20 minutes. Sprinkle over the top:

1 cup shredded soy mozzarella cheese

Bake 10 minutes longer or until the cheese has melted.

*yields 6 to 8
servings*

per serving:
calories 495
protein 21 g
fat 13 g
carb 76 g
fiber 9 g
sodium 510 mg

asian roasted vegetables
with soybeans and linguine

Preheat the oven to 350°F.

Steam for 5 minutes:

> 1 small head Napa cabbage, trimmed and quartered lengthwise

Drain well. Arrange the cabbage in two roasting pans or on two cookie sheets along with:

> 10 ounces whole mushrooms, cut in half
> ½ pound (8 ounces) asparagus, cut into bite-size pieces
> 2 red bell peppers, cut into bite-size pieces
> 6 scallions, cut into 1-inch pieces

Combine in a blender:

> ¼ cup toasted sesame seeds
> ¼ cup fresh lime juice
> 3 tablespoons tamari
> 2 tablespoons minced fresh gingerroot
> 2 tablespoons rice vinegar
> 2 tablespoons canola oil
> 1 tablespoon Chinese chili paste
> 4 cloves garlic, chopped

*This delicious blend of toasted sesame seeds and
vegetables with soybeans can be served hot or
cold as a salad. It is a real treat.*

Process until smooth, and pour evenly over the vegetables. Roast in
the oven for 15 minutes. Stir and turn over with a spatula and continue roasting 15 minutes longer.

Cook in boiling water:

½ pound (8 ounces) linguine

When the linguine is almost tender, add:

1½ cups cooked soybeans

Finish cooking until the linguine is al dente. Drain and transfer to a
large bowl. Add the roasted vegetables and the juices from the
roasting pan. Toss well and serve.

yields 6 servings

per serving:

calories 270
protein 16 g
fat 13 g
carb 29 g
fiber 8 g
sodium 592 mg

white and green beans
with pasta in orange sauce

Fresh green beans will attract you to this dish, which exemplifies the versatility of pasta meals.

Cook in a large pot of boiling water for 5 minutes:

> 10 ounces bite-size pasta (rotini, penne, rigatoni)

Add:

> 3 cups cut green beans

Cook for 5 minutes longer. Drain and transfer to a large serving bowl.

Sauté in a medium skillet for 1 to 2 minutes:

> 1½ tablespoons minced garlic
> 1 teaspoon olive oil

Stir in:

> 1½ cups chopped fresh or canned tomatoes
> 1 cup orange juice
> 1 tablespoon grated orange zest
> 1 tablespoon balsamic vinegar
> 1 teaspoon ground sage
> salt to taste

Simmer for 2 minutes. Then stir in:

> 2 cups cooked cannellini or Great Northern beans

Cook for 5 minutes. Pour over the reserved pasta and greens beans and toss well. Garnish with:

> ½ cup chopped scallions

yields 6 servings

per serving:

calories 319
protein 14 g
fat 2 g
carb 63 g
fiber 9 g
sodium 11 mg

white bean
pasta fagioli

This quick and easy dish is a favorite with the kids. Enjoy it any time of the year.

Have ready:

> 4 cups cooked small shells or elbow macaroni

In a large skillet, sauté for 5 minutes:

> 1 cup diced carrots
>
> ½ cup chopped onions
>
> ½ cup chopped celery
>
> 1 teaspoon olive oil

Stir in:

> 1 cup fresh or canned chopped tomatoes
>
> 1 teaspoon garlic powder
>
> ½ teaspoon salt (optional)
>
> ¼ teaspoon pepper

Cook for 5 minutes. Then stir in the reserved pasta along with:

> 2 cups cooked white beans (Great Northern or cannellini)

Cover and cook on low heat, stirring occasionally, until heated through.

yields 5 servings

per serving:

calories 246

protein 11 g

fat 2 g

carb 47 g

fiber 8 g

sodium 24 mg

kidney beans and veggies
over polenta cakes

Preheat the oven to 350°F.

Lightly oil a 12-cup muffin pan and set aside.

Whisk together in a medium saucepan:

> 3½ cups water
> 1 cup polenta (coarse corn meal)

Bring to a boil, stirring often, then reduce the heat and simmer, whisking frequently, for 10 minutes or until the polenta thickens. Pour equally into the prepared muffin tin (about ½-inch thick per muffin cup) and bake for 20 minutes. Remove from oven and let rest for 10 minutes before inverting onto a clean surface or removing each one with a flat table knife.

While the polenta is cooking, heat in a medium skillet:

> 2 teaspoons olive oil

When hot, add:

> 1 onion, coarsely chopped
> 2 carrots, cut into ½-inch chunks
> 1 green bell pepper, diced
> 1 red bell pepper, diced
> ¼ cup pimentos

Cover and cook over medium heat for 3 to 4 minutes, stirring occasionally. Add:

> 3 cups chopped mushrooms
> 2 zucchini, sliced in ¼-inch rounds

Enjoy these crispy, chewy polenta cakes topped with an unexpected combination of herbs, spices, beans, and vegetables.

Cover and cook 5 minutes. Stir in:

> 1½ cups cooked kidney beans
>
> 3 tablespoons fresh lemon juice
>
> 1 teaspoon dried thyme
>
> 1 teaspoon paprika
>
> 1 teaspoon ground ginger
>
> 1 teaspoon ground cumin
>
> ¼ teaspoon ground cinnamon

Cook for 2 minutes, then season with:

> salt and pepper to taste

Cover, remove from the heat, and let rest about 5 minutes before serving over the polenta cakes.

yields 4 to 6 servings

per serving:

calories 222

protein 9 g

fat 3 g

carb 42 g

fiber 8 g

sodium 24 mg

black-eyed peas
with cauliflower and sweet potatoes

This eye-catching, orange-colored dish has a hint of fennel.

Heat in a large skillet:

> 2 teaspoons olive oil

When hot, add:

> 1 head cauliflower, cut into bite-size florets
>
> 4 cups peeled and cubed sweet potatoes
>
> 1 onion, chopped
>
> 2 carrots, cut on the diagonal
>
> 3 cloves garlic, minced

Cover and cook for 15 minutes, stirring occasionally. Then stir in:

> 2 cups cooked black-eyed peas
>
> 2 cups tomato purée
>
> ⅓ cup orange marmalade
>
> 1 tablespoon grated fresh gingerroot, or 2 teaspoons ground ginger
>
> 1 tablespoon rice vinegar
>
> 1 teaspoon whole fennel seeds, crushed
>
> 1 teaspoon ground coriander
>
> ½ teaspoon ground allspice
>
> ⅛ teaspoon cayenne

Simmer for 5 minutes longer. Remove from the heat and keep covered until ready to serve over basmati rice.

yields 6 servings

per serving:

calories 298

protein 9 g

fat 3 g

carb 62 g

fiber 13 g

sodium 165 mg

sweet 'n sour
garbanzo medley

PINEAPPLE SAUCE: Drain and reserve the juice and fruit from:

> 1 (20-ounce) can pineapple chunks in unsweetened juice

Combine the pineapple juice in a medium bowl with:

> ⅓ cup apple cider vinegar
> ¼ cup sweetener of your choice
> 3 tablespoons cornstarch
> ½ teaspoon garlic powder

Stir well. Add the reserved pineapple chunks and set aside.

In a large skillet, sauté for 5 minutes:

> 2 cups sliced zucchini
> 1 cup diced carrots
> 1 bell pepper, cut into thin strips
> ¾ cup chopped onions
> ½ tablespoon grated fresh gingerroot
> 1 teaspoon canola oil

Stir in:

> 2 cups cooked garbanzo beans
> 2 cups mung bean sprouts
> ¼ cup water
> 1 to 2 tablespoons tamari

Cover and simmer for 10 minutes. Uncover and add the pineapple mixture, stirring constantly until the mixture thickens and comes to a boil. Cover and remove from the heat. Serve hot over rice or millet.

yields 6 servings

per serving:

calories 231
protein 8 g
fat 2 g
carb 48 g
fiber 5 g
sodium 267 mg

black bean winter squash
enchiladas

Preheat the oven to 350°F.

Have ready:

    10 corn tortillas

    ¾ cup shredded white soy cheese

    1 (9 x 13-inch) glass baking dish

Combine in a medium saucepan or pressure cooker:

    1 cup water

    5 dried red chili peppers, seeds removed

Boil for 15 minutes or pressure cook for 5 minutes. Remove ½ cup of the cooking water and place it in a blender or food processor along with the cooked chili peppers. Blend into a thick sauce and set aside.

In a small skillet sauté until soft and starting to brown:

    1 onion, chopped   1 teaspoon olive oil

Combine in a medium bowl:

    1¾ cups cooked winter squash (butternut, Hubbard, acorn)

    1½ cups cooked black beans

Mash well using a potato masher or fork. Add the sautéed onions and:

    3 cups salsa verde (tomatillo sauce)   salt to taste

Tomatillos are an unusual ingredient for many Americans, but they are an important part of traditional Mexican cuisine. They are little green tomatoes encased in a papery husk, and they make a delicious, mild green sauce. You can find green sauce already prepared in the Mexican food section of most supermarkets or you can make your own, if you're so inclined.

Pour 1 cup of the tomatillo sauce over the bottom of the baking dish. Prepare the tortillas by heating each one on a lightly oiled skillet, turning once. Heat them just until soft, not crisp. As each tortilla is heated, fill it with the bean and squash mixture, using ⅓ cup for each one, and roll tightly. Place in the casserole dish seam side down. When all the enchiladas are in the casserole dish, pour the remaining 2 cups of tomatillo sauce over them. Sprinkle with shredded soy cheese and bake for 30 to 40 minutes.

yields 5 servings

per serving:

calories 333
protein 14 g
fat 8 g
carb 55 g
fiber 14 g
sodium 195 mg

sweets and desserts

tutti-fruity *bars*

This is a chewy fruit bar that is good for breakfast or as a snack. It keeps well in the refrigerator.

In a food processor, combine and process until smooth:

1 ripe banana

1 cup cooked soybeans

¾ cup figs

¾ cup applesauce

½ cup orange juice

⅓ cup maple syrup or rice syrup

2 tablespoons canola oil

1 teaspoon vanilla

The figs will stay chunky. Pour into a mixing bowl.

Preheat the oven to 350°F. Sift into the mixing bowl:

3 cups unbleached white flour

1 teaspoon baking powder

1 teaspoon baking soda

¼ teaspoon salt

Stir into the wet mixture. Pour into a lightly oiled 9 x 13-inch pan, and bake for 25 minutes. Cut into pieces when cool.

yields 20 pieces

per serving:

calories 132

protein 4 g

fat 2 g

carb 25 g

fiber 2 g

sodium 109 mg

more fabulous beans

aduki carob
cake

In a food processor, combine:

> 1 cup cooked aduki beans
> ¾ cup maple syrup or rice syrup
> ½ cup soymilk
> 3 tablespoons canola oil
> 1 teaspoon vanilla extract

Blend together until smooth, and pour into a mixing bowl.

Sift into the bowl of blended liquid ingredients:

> 1½ cups flour
> ½ cup carob powder
> 1 teaspoon baking powder
> ¼ teaspoon salt

Beat or whisk the ingredients together until a smooth batter is formed. Pour into a lightly oiled, 9-inch square cake pan, and bake for 25 minutes.

yields 8 servings

per serving:

calories 240
protein 5 g
fat 5 g
carb 45 g
fiber 3 g
sodium 106 mg

sweet bean
pie

From San Francisco to New York, these pies are sold as little tarts by Muslim street vendors. If you use more oil the crust will be less chewy and more flaky.

CRUST—With a fork, mix together:

½ cup whole wheat flour

½ cup unbleached white flour

⅓ cup water

2 tablespoons canola oil

1 teaspoon sesame seeds

⅛ teaspoon salt

Work the dough with your hands until a smooth ball forms. Add more water if the dough is too dry or tends to break when you are rolling it out. Add more flour if the dough is too sticky. On a floured board, roll out the dough into a circle about 13 inches in diameter. Move the crust into a 9-inch pie pan, turn the outer edge under, and press it with a fork or make a fluted design with your fingers. Put the crust aside until the filling is ready.

Preheat the oven to 350°F.

Combine in a blender until creamy:

3 cups cooked white beans

1⅓ cups low-fat or regular soymilk

⅔ cup maple syrup or rice syrup

2 tablespoons unbleached white flour

1 teaspoon cinnamon

½ teaspoon vanilla extract

½ teaspoon ground ginger

¼ teaspoon cloves

⅛ teaspoon salt

yields 8 servings

per serving:

calories 273

protein 9 g

fat 4 g

carb 50 g

fiber 58 g

sodium 85 mg

Pour into the unbaked pie shell, and bake for 45 minutes. Cool before serving.

glossary

BALSAMIC VINEGAR A dark, rich, aged vinegar made from white grapes

BASMATI RICE Long grain rice with a nutty aroma

BLACKSTRAP MOLASSES A dark cane syrup that contains several B vitamins and minerals and is rich in iron

BULGUR Quick-cooking crushed wheat that has been steamed and dried

CHICKPEA FLOUR Also known as besan, a flour made from cooked, dried chickpeas

COUSCOUS A quick-cooking grain made from cracked semolina wheat.

LIQUID SWEETENERS These can be cane molasses, maple syrup, barley malt, brown rice syrup, etc.

MILLET A small, round, white grain. Millet develops a good flavor when it is toasted in a dry skillet before it is cooked. When added to soups, it thickens the soup by absorbing liquid. Millet is the only grain that is alkaline (acid-neutralizing) when cooked.

MISO A salty paste made from soybeans (and sometimes grains) which have been cooked and aged. Miso can be light, medium, or dark in color and can be used as a base for soups, salad dressings, and dips. The enzymes present in miso can aid digestion if they have not been boiled, so add it at the end of cooking.

NONDAIRY YOGURT Yogurt made from nondairy milk, such as soymilk, rice milk, or almond milk. Good for people with dairy allergies.

NUTRITIONAL YEAST An inactive yeast that is high in B vitamins and protein. Nutritional yeast is yellow and has a pleasant, cheesy flavor. It should not to be confused with brewer's yeast, which is bitter, or active dry yeast (baking yeast), which is used to make bread rise. It makes a wonderful condiment, sprinkled over soup.

PEARL BARLEY Hulled barley with the bran removed

RICE SYRUP A light, sweet syrup usually made from brown rice

RICE VINEGAR A mild vinegar made from fermented rice

TAHINI A smooth paste made by grinding roasted or raw sesame seeds

TAMARI A rich, flavorful high-quality soy sauce

TEXTURED VEGETABLE PROTEIN Made from extruded, defatted soy flour which has been cooked under pressure. It is dry and must be rehydrated. Textured vegetable protein can be used as a quick-to-cook replacement for ground beef. You can find it in the freezer section of some supermarkets as vegetarian crumbles or order it from The Mail Order Catalog P.O. Box 180, Summertown, TN 38483 (800-695-2241).

TURBINADO SUGAR Raw sugar (from processed sugar cane after the molasses has been removed) that has been steamed to remove impurities

VEGETARIAN WORCESTERSHIRE SAUCE Any brand of Worcestershire sauce that does not contain anchovies

index

BOOK PUBLISHING COMPANY

since 1974—books that educate, inspire, and empower

To find your favorite vegetarian and soyfood products online, visit:
www.healthy-eating.com

Soup's On!
Barb Bloomfield
1-57067-047-1 $10.95

The Ultimate Uncheese
Cookbook
Joanne Stepaniak
1-57067-151-6 $15.95

The Fiber for Life Cookbook
Bryanna Grogan
1-57067-134-6 $12.95

The Whole Foods Diabetic Cookbook
Patricia Stevenson & Michael Cook
Nutrition information by
Patricia Bertron, RD
1-57067-129-X $12.95

The New Becoming Vegetarian
Vesanto Melina, RD
Brenda Davis, RD
1-57067-144-3 $19.95

Living in the Raw
Rose Lee Calabro
1-57067-148-6 $19.95

Purchase these health titles and cookbooks from your local bookstore or
natural food store, or you can buy them directly from:

Book Publishing Company • P.O. Box 99 • Summertown, TN 38483
1-800-695-2241

Please include $3.95 per book for shipping and handling.